Causes and Cures of Welfare

Causes and Cures of Welfare

New Evidence
on the Social
Psychology
of the Poor

Leonard Goodwin
Worcester Polytechnic Institute

LexingtonBooks
D.C. Heath and Company
Lexington, Massachusetts
Toronto

Library of Congress Cataloging in Publication Data

Goodwin, Leonard, 1929–
    Causes and cures of welfare.

    Includes index.
      1. Welfare recipients—United States—Psychology.
2. Public welfare—United States.   3. Poor—United
States—Psychology.   4. Social psychology—United
States. I. Title.
HV91.G58 1983   362.5′01′9   82–48634
ISBN 0–669–06370–3

Copyright © 1983 by D.C. Heath and Company

Published simultaneously in Canada

Printed in the United States of America

International Standard Book Number: 0–669–06370–3

Library of Congress Catalog Card Number: 82–48634

To
Jack Newman and Merwin Hans,
former civil servants who recognized
the need for social research to inform
public policy.

Contents

Figures

Tables

Foreword

Now more than at any other time in our nation's history, the U.S. welfare system is under attack. Its image is badly tarnished. The reason is frustration—frustration of the American public with persistently large welfare rolls despite years of government efforts to reduce them. The taxpayers' patience with ineffectual, albeit well–intentioned, welfare policies is wearing thin.

And understandably so. All too often federal programs have failed to deliver what they promise. They have failed to help welfare recipients toward economic independence and upward mobility. In some instances, they have actually worsened the problem by further demoralizing the people they are supposed to help.

Public discontent with welfare surfaced particularly during the 1980 elections. President Reagan ran on a platform of eliminating "fraud and abuse" from the welfare system, a slogan that has translated into broad cutbacks of social services during his administration. In the same year conservatives ousted a number of senators and congressmen from office partly by branding them as bleeding hearts on welfare.

The new antiwelfare coalition has left its mark. Despite all the talk about only knocking the malingerers and deadbeats off the rolls while keeping a safety net for the truly needy, the conservatives have been pressing willy-nilly for deeper and deeper cuts. They have already succeeded in slashing such items as food stamps, Aid for Dependent Children, Medicaid and school lunches. They are calling for cuts still deeper.

In my view welfare programs that work, that provide needy Americans with the essentials of life or that provide recipients with the means to escape their misfortune, ought to stay on the books. But I am against programs that are ineffectual, that merely throw money here and there without anything to show for it. For example, I did not mourn the passing of the Comprehensive Employment and Training Act (CETA). Its implementation was riddled with political cronyism and nepotism. It had the unfortunate effect of discrediting many worthy government programs.

The CETA program provided job training for the hard-core unemployed. I agree with the premise that job training is the best solution for this nagging problem. But job training must be realistic; it must take into account the strengths and weaknesses of the people to be trained. The success of a job-training program in Bangladesh, where literacy is only 29 percent, may hinge on teaching people first to read and write. Similarly, training someone to be a carpenter will fail if the trainee lacks basic math skills and the program teaches only hammering and sawing. If a mother cannot afford to devote herself to learning a full-time job without day care for her children, then a job-training program for her ought to provide day care.

The conservatives' approach to welfare and unemployment is typically cavalier. If the economy improves, they reason, there will be jobs aplenty for everyone willing to work. Such wishful thinking is blind to the real causes behind welfare dependence: such deep-seated deficiencies as lack of skills and lack of self-confidence. Unless we tailor our remedies to the real causes, efforts to break the dependence on welfare are likely to be futile.

In *Causes and Cures of Welfare,* Professor Leonard Goodwin seeks to identify the real causes behind welfare. He does not merely presume to know what the pitfalls are, he looks to the best source for discovering them. He surveys the recipients themselves. He plumbs the psychology of the recipients and explores the reason for defeatism that afflicts them.

The book presents an array of facts and figures about the welfare system and its recipients. More importantly, it studies the attitudes of recipients and analyzes the implications for policy.

Professor Goodwin reaffirms what many suspect intuitively about welfare recipients: they are like other people in desiring to earn a decent wage and provide a better life for their children. He concludes, further, that make—work jobs and half—baked training provide no escape from welfare in the long run.

What he stresses is the value of realistic job training, both for factory workers with outmoded skills and for welfare recipients. Training is realistic when it leads to skills for which there is a demand in the local market; when the potential for employment is long range; when the prospective job offers some hope for advancement; and when the training program is buttressed by necessary support services such as child care.

This book attempts no all-encompassing answers to all questions about welfare. Professor Goodwin, however, asks many of the right questions, and he asks them of the right people. His findings point toward realistic programs that have some chance of success.

The nation can use this strong tonic of realism applied to its welfare policies. If we hoodwink ourselves into thinking that the problems will solve themselves or if we fail to fashion programs to deal with the real causes behind welfare and to break the cycle that perpetuates welfare from generation to generation, we will pay a heavy toll in the continuing social disintegration of millions of Americans. The longer we wait, the higher the toll will be.

Paul E. Tsongas
Senator from Massachusetts

Acknowledgments

This study was made possible by the belief of two civil servants, now retired, that welfare policy could benefit from research knowledge. These two are Merwin Hans, former director of the national office of the Work Incentive (WIN) Program, and Jack Newman, formerly with the Office of Research and Development. Their years of effort at the U.S. Department of Labor have earned my appreciation and that of many other social scientists who had the pleasure of working with them.

Members of my advisory committee have been an invaluable source of advice, support, and encouragement at all stages of the research; my thanks to Edgar Borgatta, David Horner, Phyllis Moen, and Leonard Pearlin. I also wish to thank Joseph Tu for his advice on the study and on the use of his INSTAT statistical package and Julie Wilson for her help in the early part of the research. The efforts of Gordon Berlin in commenting on the study and managing administrative aspects of the grant in the Department of Labor are very much appreciated.

The study could not have been completed without the excellent cooperation of the managers and staffs of the WIN program and unemployment insurance offices in Chicago and New York City. The cooperation of the fathers and mothers who provided the data necessary for this study was exceptionally gracious. The organization and supervision of the reinterview effort by Sidney Hollander and Marilee Considine of Hollander, Cohen Associates was especially commendable, as was the effort of Lieberman Research Suburban in carrying out the initial interviews. The help of Terry Williams and Phyllis Moen in completing some of the group interviews is gratefully acknowledged.

A major part of any effort such as this is careful organizing and checking of data. Carolyn Pike performed heroic deeds in this regard. Her subsequent work on the manuscript was indispensable. William LeDoux spent many hours creating computer data files and helping with the analysis. His painstaking work is very much appreciated. The research assistance of Lester Birenbaum, Deborah Chichlowski, Corene Crozier, Steven King, and Eric Milner was of great importance. Allan Johannesen was especially helpful in making available the space needed for statistical analysis on the Worcester Polytechnic Institute computer system. Jayne Nickel and Diane Geary patiently typed final copies of the manuscript.

The data reported here were gathered under Grant Number 5I–25–77–05 from the Employment and Training Administration of the U.S. Department of Labor. The views and interpretations of the author do not necessarily represent those of the Department of Labor or others associated with the study. The author alone takes responsibility for any deficiencies in the analysis or interpretations.

1

Psychological Assumptions and Welfare Policy

The orientation of Americans toward the poor is ambivalent. There is willingness to help those who are unable to help themselves, but hostility toward those who are seen as too lazy to work their way to economic independence. This ambivalence is reflected in the changing social welfare policies of the past twenty years. During the 1960s, policymakers and the general public were willing to provide a measure of help to the poor through welfare benefits, supportive services, and job training. Now benefits are being slashed and requirements are being imposed to work off any benefits that are received. We are at the far end of a policy swing dominated by the view that welfare rolls are clogged with malingerers and that government support for the poor is destroying the ability of these people to achieve economic independence.

Are current assumptions about the poor correct? Are present social welfare policies in the national interest? This book answers those queries on the basis of new knowledge. It illuminates the social and psychological reasons why some heads of households remain dependent on public welfare while others achieve economic independence. It also illuminates the impact of public welfare on marital disruption among two-parent families. For comparison, the reasons affecting the levels of economic independence and marital disruption among low-income persons applying for unemployment insurance are also examined. This new knowledge about human action provides a vantage point from which to view the adequacy of past and present welfare policies and to look forward to new policies that will remove the underlying causes of economic dependency in this country.

To place our empirical findings in policy perspective, we briefly examine the evolution of public welfare policy, the assumptions underlying current policy, and previous sources of knowledge about the social psychology of the poor.

Welfare In Perspective

The focus of our concern is public welfare provided to families with dependent children. Federally subsidized welfare of this kind was first provided under the Social Security Act of 1935. Unlike other provisions of that Act, Aid to Dependent Children (ADC) was regarded as a minor effort.[1] The target group was children who had become economically dependent because of the deaths of their fathers. The implicit theory was that the number of families headed by women, primarily widows at that time, would remain small and that these mothers should remain at home rather than trying to achieve economic independence in the labor market.

The 1962 Reform

The welfare situation changed drastically over the years. By 1962 the welfare rolls had expanded considerably. Children were found to be dependent not because of the deaths of their fathers but because the fathers had left the families or had never been part of the family unit. The welfare problem had shifted to one of family "disorganization" engendered by the presumed psychological instability of the parents.[2] The new family concern of the legislators was emphasized in the agreement to change the name of the program from Aid to Dependent Children to its current title, Aid to Families with Dependent Children (AFDC).

Congressional concern was not only for the plight of poor families, but also for the costs incurred in helping these families. There was recognition of the need to free people from long-term dependency to prevent massive social maintenance costs in the future.[3] Statutory regulations in the 1962 welfare amendments emphasized the provision of social services, including child care, to welfare families so mothers could go to work.

Provision of a vast social service effort would have required great numbers of trained social workers. The legislation talked of providing more training to develop such workers, but neither the funds nor the effort materialized. In spite of these difficulties, if provision of social services were a valid solution to the welfare problem—if it would move large number of welfare recipients toward economic independence—then whatever social services were made available should have shown some success. Instead, increased numbers of "disorganized" families came on to the welfare rolls and costs continued to climb. Table 1–1 shows the rise in numbers of welfare families, from 0.8 million in 1960 to 3.78 million in 1980.

The 1967 Reform

A further effort at reform emerged in 1967. It represented another shift in theory as to the cause of welfare dependency. Emphasis was given to

Table 1–1
Number of Families on AFDC and Federal Cost
(1960–1980)

	1960	1965	1970	1972	1974	1976	1978	1979	1980[a]
Families on AFDC (millions)	0.80	1.05	2.55	3.12	3.32	3.59	3.49	3.56	3.78
Cash Payments to AFDC Families ($billions)	1.00	1.66	4.85	6.91	7.92	10.14	10.73	11.07	12.81

Note: Data for this table, except where noted, come from *Statistical Abstracts of the United States, 1980*. Washington, D.C.: Department of Commerce, Bureau of the Census, table 570–71, p. 354.

[a]These data come from *Monthly Benefit Statistics*, note 6, July 24, 1981. Washington, D.C.: U.S. Department of Health and Human Services, Social Security Administration.

human capital development in the form of work training; thus, the Work Incentive (WIN) Program was inaugurated.[4] Local welfare offices were required to refer their clients to local WIN offices that came under the jurisdiction of state employment services.

WIN not only was to provide human-capital improvement through training, but it also offered extensive counseling services for participants. These services recognized again that welfare families had special social and psychological difficulties. Child-care efforts were expanded. In addition, "job developers" were attached to WIN offices to locate appropriate positions for WIN graduates.

As WIN was implemented, numerous administrative difficulties were encountered. The cooperation of social welfare and employment service agencies across the country was mixed. The funding for WIN was small, amounting to only about $300 million per year during a time when more than 2 million families were on welfare. But even with these limitations, if work training was the solution to welfare dependency, some success should have been noticed. From 1967 to 1970, however, the welfare rolls were growing, not shrinking.

Disillusionment set in with the human-capital approach to lowering welfare rolls, even as earlier there was disillusionment with the social-services approach. It was felt that resources for training lessened the rapidity with which welfare recipients could enter the labor market.

From 1971 to 1981

A modified strategy was proposed in the so-called Talmadge Amendments of 1971.[5] WIN offices were required to spend at least one-third of their funds for on-the-job training or public-service employment. The new theory was that placement in these components would improve the chances of participants getting regular jobs at the end of their assignments. It was also believed that welfare recipients lacked motivation to enter the work force and needed to be pushed into it. WIN staff were perceived as too easy on participants, too willing to provide training and counseling rather than forcing participants to go out and get a job.

It soon became apparent that the Talmadge Amendments were not going to turn WIN into the solution of the welfare problem. Goodwin's 1977 analysis of research on WIN showed, indeed, that WIN had a positive effect in helping welfare recipients enter the work force only when some form of training was involved. The analysis also indicated that the positive effect of WIN could not be expected to be large enough to deplete the welfare rolls markedly.[6]

While the Talmadge Amendments were being passed, President

Nixon's welfare reform package, called the Family Assistance Plan, was under consideration in Congress. The plan proposed a low-level guaranteed income. The proposal was eventually abandoned as it was impossible to find a compromise between the liberals' demand for a higher guarantee level and conservatives' opposition to any guarantee at all.[7] In 1978, President Carter proposed a welfare reform package that included the government as the employer of last resort.[8] It was never passed, rejected in part because of its presumed high cost. In 1980, when Ronald Reagan ran for president, the federal government was making direct cash payments of $12.8 billion to 3.78 million AFDC families. Eighteen years of effort at welfare reform had failed to lower welfare rolls and costs.

It is against this backdrop of failure that policies of the Reagan administration must be viewed. Those policies were passed by Congress during the summer of 1981, almost unnoticed amidst the clamor surrounding budget cuts and tax cuts.[9] They embody conservatives' assumptions about the motivation of welfare recipients and the role of the federal government in trying to help them. It is important to delineate these assumptions explicitly so that their validity can be tested against our research findings.

Conservatives View the Poor

George Gilder, a prominent conservative spokesman who has been called the leading social theorist of capitalism today, sees poor men as psychological weaklings corrupted by the welfare system.[10] He bases his analysis not only on theoretical considerations, but upon experiences he had had with poor persons in Albany, New York. In his 1978 book, *Visible Man,* Gilder tells the real-life story of Sam, a single black male in his twenties, who is content to live on the money provided him by welfare mothers.[11] Sam is content to drink and loaf rather than work to support his family. As Gilder notes:

> Sam still wants to marry and work. He wants to support his children. He would if he had to. He would if they needed him. Instead, welfare takes care of his children.[12]

Gilder sees men trapped in the ghetto because they fail to accept the discipline of family responsibility and fail to take advantage of the job opportunities available to them. For the government to offer help in this situation is seen as counterproductive and even immoral. Thus, Gilder notes in his 1981 book on wealth and poverty:

> The most serious fraud is committed not by the member of the welfare

culture, but by the creators of it, who conceal from the poor . . . that
to live well and escape from poverty they will have to keep their families together at all costs and will have to work harder than the classes
above them. In order to succeed, the poor need most of all the spur of
their poverty.[13]

The presumed psychological insight into the poor that Gilder offers
is extremely attractive to the rich. It relieves them of feelings of guilt or
social responsibility. People are poor because they have been overin-
dulged by benefits provided by taxing the rich. The policy implications
of such a view are clear and simple: lower welfare benefits and require
hard work for whatever payments are given. This is indeed the policy of
the Reagan administration. Programs for the poor have been slashed and
the states are encouraged to require welfare recipients to work for their
welfare benefits—to implement what is called "workfare."[14] The 1982–
1983 budget proposed by the president would require the imposition of
workfare.

Robert Carleson, a special assistant to President Reagan, emphasizes
the need for persons to work for their welfare checks:

> Able-bodied welfare recipients should be required to work in useful
> public employment for their benefits until they are able to find work
> in the private sector.[15]

Carleson rationalizes the importance of work requirements in the
same terms as Gilder: namely, the need to prevent poor people from
succumbing to their psychological weakness of accepting handouts rather
than working. Thus, Carleson notes:

> The American people do not expect their welfare system to provide
> benefits to those who will not help themselves. The message of the
> recent welfare work requirement in Bordentown, New Jersey, is that
> able-bodied welfare recipients will find jobs when it is made clear that
> they are expected to earn their benefits. In Bordentown, confronted
> with the work requirement, twenty-three of the twenty-six people who
> had been on welfare dropped from the rolls.[16]

Carleson substantiates his view of the psychological weakness of welfare
recipients on the basis of twenty-six cases in a small New Jersey town.
Gilder supports a similar view on the basis of experiences with a few
poor people in Albany, New York. Surely one would hope to have more
substantial psychological knowledge than that for shaping policies and
programs that affect the lives of millions of people. One might expect
to find more substantial knowledge in the scholarly community. What

have social scientists discovered about the psychology of poor people on welfare?

Previous Research Studies

Recipients of public welfare, including those who receive AFDC, have not been the favorite research subjects of psychologists, sociologists, or social psychologists. There is relatively little empirical data on the psychology and behavior of welfare recipients. Most efforts of behavioral scientists center around middle-class persons and institutions.[17] The data that do exist indicate that AFDC recipients are as committed to supporting their families through work as are regularly employed persons. When welfare recipients differ from more affluent persons with respect to certain viewpoints—for example, in showing less confidence in their ability to succeed—the results can be attributed to their less favorable experiences in the work world.[18] These earlier studies, however, do not establish the causes of recipients' behaviors. They do not indicate why some welfare recipients achieve economic independence through work while others remain dependent. Also, the issue of marital stability among AFDC families headed by men has not been adequately addressed.

If social scientists in certain fields have tended to ignore the welfare poor, others in economics have been concerned with them. Three studies carried out over a period of years by economists will be examined briefly for their relevance to understanding the behavior of poor people.

University of Michigan Study

A continuing study of 5,000 families including low-income families who have been on and off welfare has been directed by economists at the University of Michigan since 1968.[19] This Panel Study of Income Dynamics focused on the reasons for changes in the economic status of these families from year to year. Data were collected primarily on the background characteristics of family members and their sources of income.

The researchers did not develop any guiding theory or model of how social psychological processes—that is, the interaction between people's views and experiences—might relate to economic achievement. They merely introduced a few social psychological measures—such as feelings of self-confidence, planning for future events, and trust in other people—that had been used in other research contexts. It is not too surprising that their psychological measures had little or no ability to predict subsequent earnings of respondents. The researchers found that the major impact on earnings came from background characteristics such as level of education.[20]

Data from the University of Michigan study also allowed prediction of marital separation. Significant reasons for separation included the father's loss of a job or an otherwise sudden loss of income.[21] These reasons, while statistically significant, were not very powerful in explaining the amount of separation observed. No significant effects of the social psychological measures were reported. (Apparently no relevant questions were asked about the quality of the marital relationships.)

We do not mean to detract from the overall significance of the University of Michigan Study. It does provide a rich source of empirical data on the economic experiences of familes and their members. Unfortunately, the study tells us virtually nothing about the social psychological experiences of respondents.

Ohio State University Study

Another continuing study (the National Longitudinal Surveys) directed by economists, has been conducted at Ohio State University since 1966. Respondents are a national sample of men and women in certain age groups. The study's aim has been to consider the work history of respondents, their work experiences, and changes in certain attitudes toward work and self in relation to labor force participation.[22] Although not directly relevant to welfare recipients, the study provides additional insight into the use of social, psychological, and background measures in predicting economic achievement.

The analysis of data particularly emphasized the social psychological variable that deals with confidence in one's ability to achieve goals. This variable was found to affect the job incomes of youths. Its impact, however, was very small. Young people with a strong sense of confidence earned only a few cents more per hour than those with a weak sense of confidence.[23]

Another very small impact on youths' earnings came from the expectation of achieving certain occupational levels.[24] The significant impacts on earnings, as with the University of Michigan Study, came from such background characteristics as level of education. Although this study provides important data on the work experiences of major segments of the American population, it does not satisfactorily illuminate the psychological bases for outcomes of these experiences.

Guaranteed Income Study

Economists have also recently completed a guaranteed-income experiment in Seattle and Denver.[25] Participants in the experiment included low-income heads of families who might have been eligible for welfare and persons with somewhat higher incomes. The study's main concern was to determine the effect of the income guarantee on the labor-force activity of heads of households. That is, researchers wished to know how much lower-income people would decrease the amount of time spent on work if they could recover some of the lost earnings through the income guarantee.

Using a control group of persons who received no income guarantee, along with the experimental group, it was found that over time the guarantee led to a reduction in work activity of three groups: male heads of households by as much as 10 percent; wives of these men by as much as 21 percent; and female heads of households by as much as 13 percent.[26] These findings were used by the researchers to estimate the billions of dollars that a nationwide guaranteed-income program would cost.

Costs obviously would rise as persons accepted the guarantee rather than working as much as they could. Researchers gave little attention to why certain people might be willing to reduce their work activity, merely relying on the standard economic assumption that people prefer nonwork to work if dollar income is the same in both situations. Failure to determine the social and psychological causes of action probably biased results of the experiment. The findings in chapter 4 throw into serious doubt the conclusion that differences in labor-force activity between the experimental and control groups were caused by the income guarantee.

Another concern of the Seattle-Denver experiment was the impact of an income guarantee upon marital separation. The theory invoked was that mothers tended to become more ''independent''—that is, more willing to set up their own households—as they commanded more money through the guarantee. Social psychological factors affecting marital disruption, including the quality of family relationships, were virtually ignored.[27] It was not even determined whether participants were formally married or just living together.[28]

When the empirical findings revealed that more families on the lower-income guarantee schedules had separated than expected, researchers were unable to explain why. They developed a complex mathematical formulation to rescue the view that availability of income to the mothers caused their departure from their husbands, using the only data that were available: background characteristics and employment experiences.[29]

Researchers were unable to determine whether the income guarantee allowed some mother to remove themselves and their children from destructive marital situations, whether the income guarantee encouraged some mothers and fathers to abandon frivolously their marital responsibilities, or whether feelings of stigma in accepting the guarantee caused marital disruption.[30] Findings in chapter 5 illuminate these possibilities and provide additional insight beyond the Seattle-Denver experiment into the potential impact and significance of a guaranteed income.

The point is that none of these three extensive economic studies illuminates the psychology of welfare recipients. None of them provides substantial enough data to support or controvert the psychological assumptions underlying current welfare-workfare policies. The study presented in this book helps fill this gap in our knowledge.

Purpose of This Book

This book raises and answers the following six questions:

1. Does preference for welfare or rejection of work keep welfare (AFDC) recipients out of the work force?
2. Does the welfare experience increase people's dependency on welfare?
3. Why do some recipients work their way to economic independence under current economic conditions while others continue on welfare?
4. What effect does a work-training program—the Work Incentive (WIN) Program in particular—have on participants' achievement of economic independence?
5. How does the receipt of welfare affect the marital stability of two-parent families?
6. Does the social psychology of unemployment-insurance applicants differ from that of welfare recipients with respect to achieving economic independence and marital stability?

Adequate answers to these questions can be obtained only in the course of expanding our understanding of human action. Findings from welfare recipients and the comparison groups of persons applying for unemployment insurance contribute to basic social-psychological knowledge as well as provide the basis for new social welfare policies.

Without trying to anticipate the findings presented in succeeding chapters, we can note here that the psychological assumptions of George Gilder and the Reagan administration regarding welfare recipients are oversimplifications of a more complex reality. Full consideration of the social-psychological experiences of the poor reveal the lowering of welfare benefits and imposing of workfare to be inadequate and even destructive social policies. Quite different policies are suggested by findings in this book.

Notes

1. Bruno Stein, *On Relief* (New York: Basic Books, 1971), pp. 70–71.

2. U.S. Congress, House, *Public Welfare Amendments of 1962*, H.R. 1414, 87th Cong., 2nd sess., 1962, p. 8.

3. Ibid., p. 9.

4. U.S. Congress, House, *Conference Report on Social Security Amendments of 1967*, H.R. 1030, 90th Cong., 1st sess., 1967.

5. U.S. Congress, House, *Public Law 92-223*, 92nd Cong., H.R. 10604, December 28, 1971, p. 8.

6. Leonard Goodwin, *The Work Incentive (WIN) Program and Related Experiences*, R&D Monograph 49. (Washington, D.C.: U.S. Department of Labor, Employment and Training Administration, 1977), pp. 13–18, 38.

7. See, for example, Ralph Segalman and Asoke Basu, *Poverty in America* (Westport, Conn.: Greenwood Press, 1981), p. 199.

8. U.S. Congress, Senate, *Welfare Reform Proposals*, Hearings before the Subcommittee on Public Assistance of the Senate Committee on Finance, 95th Cong., 2nd sess., 1978, pt. 1, p. 136.

9. *Congressional Record, House*, June 25, 1981, p. H3442.

10. See statement by William F. Buckley, Jr., Transcript of Public Broadcasting presentation of *Firing Line*, February 8, 1981 (Columbia, S.C.: Southern Educational Communications Association, 1981), p. 1.

11. George Gilder, *Visible Man: A True Story of Post-racist America* (New York: Basic Books, 1978).

12. Ibid., p. 246.

13. George Gilder, *Wealth and Poverty* (New York: Basic Books, 1981), p. 116.

14. *Congressional Record—House*. June 25, 1981, p. H3442.

15. Robert B. Carleson and Kevin R. Hopkins, "Whose Responsibility is Social Responsibility: The Reagan Rationale," *Public Welfare* 39 (Fall 1981), 14.

16. Ibid.

17. For a discussion of the reasons behind the lack of research on the psychology of poor youth, see Leonard Goodwin, "Poor Youth and Employment: A Social Psychological Perspective," *Youth and Society* 11 (March 1980), 311–351.

18. Goodwin, *The Work Incentive Program and Related Experiences*, p. 35.

19. Greg J. Duncan and James N. Morgan, eds. *Five Thousand*

American Families: Patterns of Economic Progress, vol. 3 (Ann Arbor, Mich.: University of Michigan, Survey Research Center, Institute for Social Research, 1975).

20. Ibid., p. 99.

21. Isabel V. Sawhill et al. *Income Transfers and Family Structure* (Washington, D.C.: Urban Institute, 1975), p. 40.

22. Paul J. Andrisani, *Work Attitudes and Labor Market Experience: Evidence from the National Longitudinal Surveys* (New York: Praeger, 1978).

23. Ibid., p. 124.

24. Ibid., p. 152.

25. Philip K. Robins et al., eds. *A Guaranteed Annual Income.* New York: Academic Press, 1980.

26. Ibid., p. 95.

27. See Leonard Goodwin. "Limitations of the Seattle and Denver Income Maintenance Analysis," *American Journal of Sociology* 85 (1979), pp. 653–657. Also see the reply by the original authors of the article referred to in the Goodwin comment: Michael T. Hannon et al., "Reply to Goodwin," ibid., 657–661.

28. Michael T. Hannon et al., "Income and Marital Events: Evidence from an Income Maintenance Experiment," *American Journal of Sociology* 82 (1977), 1195.

29. Michael T. Hannon et al., "Income and Independence Effects on Marital Dissolution," *American Journal of Sociology* 84 (1978), 611–633.

30. Goodwin. "Limitations of the Seattle and Denver Income Maintenance Analysis."

2 Setting of the Study

The validity of our empirical results and the interpretations flowing from them depend upon the validity of our procedures. This chapter outlines those procedures and the rationale for developing various measures. Details appear in the appendixes.

Samples and Sites

When this study was initiated in 1978, approximately 3.5 million heads of households were receiving AFDC. Of this group, 1.1 million were judged work-ready and were required by law to participate in the Work Incentive (WIN) program.[1] Inasmuch as our concern was with why AFDC recipients do or do not achieve economic independence, it made sense to select our sample from the WIN participants—those who could be expected to work.

An additional interest was to determine why WIN fathers as well as WIN mothers achieved economic independence. Fathers who head households constitute only 5 percent of all AFDC households and only 12 percent of all WIN registrants.[2] (These low figures partly result from the fact that only half the states, mostly in the North, allow fathers to receive welfare at all.) While small in numbers an understanding of the bases for economic independence and marital stability in these families throws important new light upon these same achievements in other low-income two-parent families.

Only the very largest northern or western cities could provide sufficient numbers of male WIN entrants for our research during the period of data collection. The results reported in the following chapters come from fathers and mothers who were entering the WIN program in New York City and Chicago during the summer of 1978.

To place results from WIN respondents in perspective, data were gathered from another set of unemployed heads of households. These were persons applying for unemployment insurance (UI) in Chicago and New York City.

The UI program, while mandated and overseen by the federal government, is financed by a tax on the payrolls of employers. Recipients of UI, therefore, are receiving benefits that accrued from their past employment. UI benefits are for a limited period of time—usually six months—whereas AFDC benefits continue as long as a person fails to have the means to support his or her children. Not all jobs are covered by the UI program. Many of the casual labor jobs performed by those people who end up receiving AFDC are not covered by UI. In general, UI recipients are eligible for higher-level jobs and are higher on the socioeconomic ladder than AFDC recipients.[3] The point of our comparison is to see if there are radically different reasons for AFDC persons achieving economic independence and marital stability than other unemployed persons applying for a different benefit program.

Initial WIN Interviews

Interviewers working for our research project were stationed at all WIN intake offices in both cities from the middle of July 1978 until October 1978. AFDC persons who were registering for WIN were referred to the interviewers by WIN intake staff. Details regarding interviews with each sample are presented in appendix A.

The questionnaire distributed to WIN participants was designed to be self-administered and required about 35 minutes to complete. The interviewers explained to respondents how to complete the questionnaire and helped them read the questionnaire as necessary. One criterion for eligibility in the study was the ability to understand (not necessarily read) English. Other criteria were that respondents be less than 61 years of age, be the head of household, and have at least one child living at home who was less than 19 years old. Male respondents had to be living with a mate, although not necessarily formally married. Each male respondent was given a questionnaire for his mate to complete and return. Results from the mates' responses are not reported in this book, except as they bear on the issue of marital disruption discussed in chapter 5. A sample questionnaire for women is presented as appendix C. A total of 814 WIN mothers and 543 WIN fathers completed usable questionnaires in 1978.

Initial UI Interviews

UI applicants were chosen for interview in the UI offices by the same criteria used for the WIN registrants. In addition, respondents were *not* to have been laid off temporarily or as part of a regular seasonal adjustment of an industry (for example, a school-bus driver). It was decided to obtain UI applicants who would be as close as possible to the socioeconomic level of AFDC recipients. The method adopted was to require each UI respondent to reside in or adjacent to a ZIP Code area where WIN persons in the study resided. To maximize the possibility of locating such UI applicants, only those UI offices close to WIN residential areas were used as sites for interviews.

Because people may apply for UI without prior screening, a certain proportion of applicants were ineligible for UI—either they had not worked long enough to qualify or their jobs were not covered by UI benefits. (WIN applicants already had been screened for welfare eligibility at welfare offices, if not already on welfare, prior to appearing at WIN offices.) Where it is appropriate in our analysis we will distinguish between UI applicants and UI recipients. A total of 245 UI mothers and 284 UI fathers completed the questionnaire during the summer and early fall of 1978.

Reinterviews

During the summer and fall of 1979 attempts were made to reinterview the 1978 WIN and UI respondents. Mail, telephone, and, in certain cases, personal visits were used to locate these persons and have them complete a second, shorter questionnaire. The main focus of the 1979 questionnaire was the work and welfare experiences of respondents and changes in marital status that occurred since the initial interview. From these data it was possible to measure marital disruption in each family that originally was headed by a male as well as each respondent's economic independence at time of reinterview and for each month between the two interviews.

A total of 428 WIN mothers and 302 WIN fathers completed the second questionnaire. The total reinterview rate was about 57 percent. (See appendix A.)

Group Interviews

During 1980 and 1981 group discussions were carried out with five groups of WIN fathers and three groups of WIN mothers who had participated in the earlier phases of the study. There were about ten persons in each group plus the social scientists. Professor Phyllis Moen helped the author with the group interviews with WIN mothers and Dr. Terry Williams helped with three of the group interviews with WIN fathers. Verbatim transcripts were made of the uninhibited discussions about work, welfare, and family relationships. (See appendix A.) In the group discussions, excerpted in succeeding chapters, the names of respondents have been altered to preserve confidentiality.

The Idea of Economic Independence

A basic aim of our study is to determine why some people continue in dependence—whether on welfare or UI—over a period of time, while others become independent. A necessary first step is to be able to measure different levels of economic independence, thereby creating a variable called economic independence. The next step is to regard economic independence as a *dependent* variable to be predicted or explained by other *independent* variables.

The dependent variable could consist of a simple measure of whether or not the respondent was on an income support program. Persons on an income-support program, however, may exhibit different levels of independence by earning different amounts of money. For example, some welfare recipients earn money through employed work (with a portion of their earnings deducted from their welfare grant). Those who work are more economically independent than those who receive their entire income from welfare.

We can realize further that persons who have left an income-support program also can be distinguished by the different amounts of money they earn. It is important to consider these earnings relative to any measure of economic independence inasmuch as the greater the earnings the less likely are persons to fall back upon an income-support program.

A useful measure of economic independence would combine consideration of being on or off an income-support program with level of earnings. The variable would have a continuous range of values: at the low end, all income derived from an income-support program; at the high end all income derived from employment.

Construction of this continuous variable is described in appendix D. A very much simpler four-point variable can be created that is strongly correlated with the continuous one and is predicted by the same independent variables. We use this simpler measure of economic independence because of its more obvious meaning (and as noted in appendix D, because we can obtain month-by-month values during the 1978–1979 period). Thus, we define economic independence through work (ECOI) as a variable with the following values:

0 = Yes income support, No work

1 = Yes income support, Yes work

2 = No income support, No work

3 = No income support, Yes work

Data gathered in the 1979 questionnaire permit us to assign a value of economic independence to each respondent. In subsequent statistical analyses, the 1979 measure of economic independence will be a dependent variable that is predicted by the 1978 independent, or predictor, variables. The term "model" or "model of economic independence" is used to indicate all the independent variables predicting economic independence. To specify the kinds of variables that are likely to predict economic independence, it is necessary to have some general hypotheses or ideas about its causes.

Kinds of Causes of Economic Independence

We view a person's level of achievement of economic independence as a result of his or her psychological orientations toward such matters as work and welfare, previous work background, the nature of the job market, and the role of federal intervention efforts such as the WIN program. The following sections describe these variables as used in the present study.

Meaning of Psychological Orientations

We adopt the term "psychological orientation" to refer to a conscious process going on within a person that orients him or her toward social actions such as going to work. Our concern is "social psychological" in the sense that we are seeking psychological explanations for persons fulfilling social patterns of activity, as distinct from primarily personal patterns of action, such as those associated with personality styles.

Although social psychologists have not focused their attention on welfare recipients as noted earlier, there is evidence to suggest the usefulness of certain kinds of measures they have developed. For example, Goodwin's earlier research showed that the work activity of a small number of welfare mothers was predicted (negatively) by one orientation expressing the expectation or intention to go on welfare.[4] Researchers in other contexts have shown the importance of the expectation, or what they call the "intention," to act as a predictor of action.[5, 6]

In addition it is intuitively reasonable that a person's expectations of achieving a goal should facilitate such achievement. With respect to welfare recipients, the achievement has two interrelated components: going to work and getting off welfare. Hence, a measure of expectation of economic independence should combine both these components and could be reasonably thought to predict such independence.

One also might consider the relevance of a person's emotional commitment or feeling toward the goal of supporting a family through work. We will use the term "attitude" to indicate this kind of feeling. A measure of welfare recipients' attitudes toward supporting a family might predict their achievement of economic independence. In a similar vein, measures of commitment to alternative forms of income such as welfare or gambling also might influence the level of economic independence achieved through work.

Attitudes toward one's mate may or may not affect one's achievement of economic independence, but such attitudes are likely to be important predictors of marital disruption, with which we also are concerned. Thus, it is useful to measure attitudes toward mates and family functioning.

Beliefs about an activity being good or bad, called "normative beliefs," also seem likely to influence action.[7, 8] If one believes that work is good and welfare is bad, one may be more likely to achieve economic independence through work than a person who believes the reverse. The more that one's family members believe work is good and welfare bad, the more a person may be influenced to go to work and avoid welfare. It is reasonable to create measures regarding these kinds of normative beliefs.

Orientations regarding self-confidence, as noted in chapter 1, have been used in past research to predict economic status. It is reasonable to measure that orientation here along with self-identification with work. Finally, it is reasonable to measure attitudes toward certain services that the WIN program might offer welfare recipients as an indicator of the seriousness of respondents' interest in leaving welfare.

Measuring Psychological Orientations

To measure these orientations more than 250 questions, or items, were written that could be rated on four-point scales—for example, a scale where 1 means Strongly Disagree and 4 means Strongly Agree. Details of the procedure for choosing the final set of items appear in appendix B. Responses to items used in the 1978 interviews were statistically analyzed to determine which items were similar to one another and so defined meaningful psychological orientations. The most relevant orientations and their component items are presented in table 2–1. The

Table 2–1
Component Items of Orientations

Orientations	Items	Rating Scale (1 to 4 steps)
I. Expectations		
1. Expect Economic Independence through Work Next Year—Mother	At this time next year how likely is it that you will be: a. Working at a fulltime job b. Receiving welfare[a] c. Staying home to look after your family[a]	Not at All Likely to Very Likely
2. Expect Economic Independence through Work Next Year—Father	At this time next year how likely is it that you will be: a. Working at a fulltime job b. Receiving welfare[a] c. Looking for a job[a]	Not at All Likely to Very Likely
3. Intend to Leave Welfare or UI if Payments Cut 10 percent	If you were on welfare, how likely would you be to go off if your welfare payments were cut by 10 percent	Not at All Likely to Very Likely
	If you were receiving unemployment compensation, how likely would you be to go off if your unemployment compensation payments were cut by 10 percent	Not at All Likely to Very Likely
II. Preference for Nonwork Income		
4. Welfare is a Good Way of Life	Give your opinion on how good a way of life it would be for you to be receiving welfare	Not Very Good Way of Life to Very Good Way of Life
5. Welfare Preferred to Work (WIN only)	When I applied for welfare this time, I felt that I would rather be on welfare than work to support my family	Strongly Disagree to Strongly Agree
6. UI Preferred to Work (UI only)	When I applied for unemployment insurance this time, I felt I would rather be on unemployment insurance than work to support my family	Strongly Disagree to Strongly Agree
7. People Malinger on Welfare or UI	a. Most people who get unemployment insurance could get another job if they really tried	Strongly Disagree to Strongly Agree

Table 2–1
Component Items of Orientations

Orientations	Items	Rating Scale (1 to 4 steps)
	b. When a person is out of work it's usually because of not looking hard enough for a new job	
	c. People get used to welfare after a while and don't want to leave	
	d. Because of welfare a lot of women are free to leave their husbands if things are bad	
	e. Most people on welfare could get off by working if they wanted to	
	f. After one month of unemployment insurance persons should be required to take any job that pays more than their unemployment benefits	
	Each item in the remainder of this section was prefaced by: How acceptable would each of these be if everyone in your family was out of work:	Each item in the remainder of this section was rated on a scale of: Not Acceptable to Very Acceptable
8. Accept Welfare when Necessary	Receiving welfare	
9. Accept UI when Necessary	Receiving unemployment insurance	
10. Accept Government Support when Necessary	a. Having the government send you enough money every week	
	b. Receiving unemployment compensation	
	c. Receiving welfare	
11. Accept Borrowing from Friends and Relatives when Necessary	a. Borrowing money from friends	
	b. Borrowing money from relatives	
12. Accept Social Security or Pension when Necessary	a. Receiving social security	

Table 2–1

Component Items of Orientations

Orientations	Items	Rating Scale (1 to 4 steps)
	b. Receiving a pension from a company where you used to work	
13. Accept Gambling when Necessary	a. Playing the numbers b. Buying lottery tickets	
III. Normative Beliefs about Work, Family, and Government Support		
14. Man Needs Job for Self-Worth	A man really can't think well of himself unless he has a job	Strongly Disagree to Strongly Agree
15. Father Should Leave Family if He Cannot Support Them	a. A man should leave his family if he cannot support them b. It is all right for a father to leave his family if they can get more money on welfare when he is gone c. Whether a family stays together is mainly a matter of lucky breaks	Strongly Disagree to Strongly Agree
16. All Right for Mother to Work	a. When children are less than 6 years old, a mother should feel free to go to work at least part-time b. When children are more than 6 years old, a mother should feel free to go to work full-time c. A woman should help her partner provide money for their family to live on	Strongly Disagree to Strongly Agree
17. Family or Neighbors Look Down on Me for Receiving Welfare or UI	a. My family would look down on me for being on unemployment insurance b. My family would look down on me for being on welfare c. My neighbors would look down on me for being on unemployment insurance d. My neighbors would look down on me for being on welfare	Strongly Disagree to Strongly Agree

Table 2–1
Component Items of Orientations

Orientations	Items	Rating Scale (1 to 4 steps)
18. Government Provide Job or Support	a. The government should guarantee a job to everybody who wants one	Strongly Disagree to Strongly Agree
	b. The government should make sure that each family has enough to live on	
	c. People who get unemployment insurance deserve it because they have worked before	
	d. People should be able to get unemployment insurance when the company they work for goes out of business	
	e. Many people are on welfare because they can't find jobs that pay enough to support their families	
IV. Family Relationships		
19. Want a Two-Parent Family—Mother	a. Having a husband who supports you and your children	Not Very Good Way of Life to Very Good Way of Life
	b. Having a family where the husband, wife, and children live together	
	c. Having a good education	
	d. Having your children get a good education	
20. Want to Support A Two-Parent Family—Father	a. Working full-time to support a family	Not Very Good Way of Life to Very Good Way of Life
	b. Having a full-time job	
	c. Having a family where the husband, wife, and children live together	
	d. Having a good education	
	e. Having plenty of money	
	f. Having your children get a good education	
21. Want Others, Not a Husband, to Support Your Family—Mother	a. Having a close man friend, not a husband, who helps support you and your children	Not Very Good Way of Life to Very Good Way of Life

Table 2–1
Component Items of Orientations

Orientations	Items	Rating Scale (1 to 4 steps)
	b. Receiving welfare	
	c. Receiving unemployment insurance	
	d. Being a single parent head of family	
22. Want Others to Support Your Family—Father	a. Having a wife who supports you and your children	Not Very Good Way of Life to Very Good Way of Life
	b. Having a close woman friend, not a wife, who helps support you and your children	
	c. Receiving welfare	
	d. Having a part-time job	
23. Family Satisfaction	a. Overall, I feel satisfied with our family the way it is now	Strongly Disagree to Strongly Agree
	b. Overall, I am satisfied with the way my children are being raised	
	c. I like the way our family handles money now	
24. Have Family Problems	A major problem our family faces is:	Strongly Disagree to Strongly Agree
	a. Handling the children	
	b. Getting along with one another	
25. Thought of Leaving Mate	I have seriously thought of leaving my mate in the last few months	Strongly Disagree to Strongly Agree
V. Self		
26. Self-Confidence	a. I can do almost anything I really set my mind to	Strongly Disagree to Strongly Agree
	b. I usually finish whatever I start	
	c. When I make plans, I am almost certain that I can make them work	
	d. I am able to do most things at least as well as other people	
	e. I am sure that life will work out all right	
27. Success through External Forces	a. In order to get ahead in a job, you need to have some lucky breaks	Strongly Disagree to Strongly Agree

Table 2–1
Component Items of Orientations

Orientations	Items	Rating Scale (1 to 4 steps)
	b. Success in a job is mainly a matter of knowing the right people	
	c. Success in life is mainly a matter of knowing the right people	
28. Self-Development Through Work	a. To me, it is important to have the kind of work that gives me a chance to develop my own special abilities	Strongly Disagree to Strongly Agree
	b. Getting recognition for my own work is important to me	
	c. I feel good when I have a job	
	d. I like to work	
	e. Success in a job is mainly a matter of hard work	
	f. Success in life comes mainly from having drive and ambition	
	g. Hard work makes you a better person	
VI. WIN Services		
29. Want WIN Help with Personal Problems	Each item in this section was prefaced by: I would like to receive these WIN services: a. Counselling about my personal affairs	Not at All to Very Much
	b. Sympathy about my situation	
	c. Help with child care arrangements	
	d. Help in transportation to a job	
30. Want WIN Advice about Getting a Job	Advice about getting a job	
31. Want WIN to Find Job	Placement in a regular job	

aThe scores on this item have been reversed so that the meaning of the item in the orientation is reversed. For example, item b in orientation 1 has its score reversed by subtracting that original score from 5; the new score is a measure of expectation to not receive welfare.

orientations are grouped into six categories on the basis of their substantive content.

The first category of orientations deals with expectations regarding economic independence through work. The first two orientations presented are similar but not identical: one is for fathers and the other for mothers. Expectation to go to work and expectation to leave welfare are components of a single orientation.

The second category, "Preference for Nonwork Income," consists of ten orientations that measure attitudes and normative beliefs regarding welfare. These orientations will be used to test the idea that many persons remain on welfare because they believe it is an acceptable form of income.

The third category, "Normative Beliefs About Work, Family, and Government Support," contains five orientations that deal with the significance of work in relation to self-esteem and family responsibilities. One orientation measures the respondent's belief about the responsibility of the government toward unemployed persons.

The fourth category, "Family Relationships," contain seven orientations that focus on belief in the two-parent family as well as feelings (attitudes) about family members. The fifth category, "Self," contains three measures dealing with the bases for success in relation to one's self or one's effort and the contribution of work to development of one's self. The sixth category, "WIN Services," contains three attitude measures regarding services that might have been obtained from the WIN program.

Most orientations are composed of two or more items. The rating, or score, obtained on an orientation is the average of the ratings given all its component items. Reliabilities of the orientations (the extent to which ratings given them are stable) are presented in appendix B.

Meaning of Background and Family Characteristics

Another way of viewing the causes of action is in terms of background characteristics of persons. These characteristics include physical attributes, skills, and achievements. Certain characteristics, such as race or gender, are bestowed without one's choice and certainly affect the kinds of things one does in society. Other characteristics develop in the course of action and experience—for example, level of education or job skills attained. Our basic dependent variable, economic independence, is a characteristic that can be altered. Background characteristics include family relationships—such as whether one is married—but those relationships have such a special meaning that we regard them as a separate set of "family characteristics."

Background and family characteristics could be seen as the fundamental causes of both psychological orientations and subsequent actions. One could maintain that a person's expectation of achieving economic independence could be completely understood in terms of his or her background such as level of education and previous job experience. Psychological orientations could be seen as having no independent effect on action. Economists and certain sociologists have adopted such a position, as noted in chapter 1. During this study, we demonstrate the limitations of such a view and show the relationships that exist among background characteristics, family characteristics, and psychological orientations with respect to affecting the achievement of economic independence (and marital stability).

The background and family characteristics that have been used in previous economic and sociological research which will be measured here, include age, educational level, race, gender, previous job pay, marital status, and total number of children in the family. Additional characteristics are mentioned in subsequent chapters, and the full set measured in this study can be seen in the 1978 questionnaire included in appendix B.

Job Market Conditions and Federal Intervention

Attaining economic independence involves not only the psychology and characteristics of individuals but the job markets these persons encounter. If there is a great demand for labor, the chances of welfare recipients working and achieving economic independence are probably greater than when there is a small demand for labor. The present analysis does not deal explicitly with differences in labor market conditions. Essentially all respondents in either Chicago or New York City are regarded as facing the same labor market conditions, while controlling for differences between the two cities in the statistical analyses.

This is not to say that we believe labor market conditions are unimportant. They are very important, as emphasized in chapter 7. But the main contribution of this study is to show the impact of welfare recipients' psychological orientations and characteristics on their achievement of economic independence and marital stability when labor-market conditions are more or less the same.

Labor-market conditions can be influenced not only by broad economic conditions and the predilections of employers, but by direct intervention of the federal government. The WIN program has been a federal effort aimed at upgrading the employability of welfare recipients so that they could achieve economic independence. We will determine the extent to which the WIN program helped welfare recipients in that regard when it located jobs for them.

The many orientations and background and family characteristics measured in this study, along with the measure of whether WIN provided jobs, become the pool of possible predictors of economic independence and marital stability of welfare recipients. The following chapters reveal the specific predictors of those outcomes and the meaning they have for welfare policy.

Notes

1. *WIN: 10th Annual Report to the Congress* (Washington, D.C.: U.S. Department of Labor and U.S. Department of Health and Human Services, 1980), p. 6.

2. Ibid., p. 27.

3. Martin S. Feldstein, "Unemployment Insurance: Time for Reform," *Harvard Business Review* (March/April 1975), 51–61.

4. Leonard Goodwin, *Do the Poor Want to Work?* (Washington, D.C.: Brookings Institution, 1972), p. 94.

5. Martin Fishbein and Icek Azjen, *Belief, Attitude and Behavior* (Reading, Mass.: Addison-Wesley, 1975).

6. Harry C. Triandis, *Interpersonal Behavior* (Monterey, Calif.: Brooks/Cole, 1977).

7. Fishbein and Ajzen, *Belief, Attitude and Behavior*.

8. Triandis, *Interpersonal Behavior*.

3 Causes of Mothers' Economic Independence

This chapter reveals why some WIN mothers achieve economic independence while others do not. It also compares results from welfare mothers with those from UI mothers. The interplay of statistical results and excerpts from group interviews with the welfare mothers adds to an understanding of the reasons for mothers achieving different levels of economic independence. Our understanding also is expanded by awareness of the characteristics of the two groups of women.

Background and Family Characteristics

Selected background and family characteristics of the mothers are presented in table 3–1. The difficulties that welfare mothers face in achieving economic independence are immediately apparent. More than half the mothers did not graduate from high school. The mothers have to support an average of 2.4 children, while their earning power is only about $118 per week. It is not surprising that only 16 percent of them achieved complete economic independence in 1979.

The UI mothers are economically better off than their welfare counterparts. More UI mothers have graduated from high school; UI mothers have fewer children to support and command higher salaries in the job market. It is reasonable, therefore, that 46 percent of the UI mothers were economically independent through work in 1979. At issue is whether the achievement of economic independence among UI or WIN mothers is solely the result of background characteristics—that is, whether mothers with more education achieve greater economic independence—or whether psychological orientations also play a role.

Economic Independence of WIN Mothers

The best set of predictors of economic independence has been determined through a statistical technique called ''regression analysis.'' This technique involves the development of an equation in which the independent variables are given certain weights (coefficients) and then added to predict the dependent variable. The equation constitutes the model of eco-

29

Table 3–1

Selected Characteristics of WIN and UI Mothers

(Means or Percentages, Standard Deviations in Parentheses)

Characteristics	WIN Mothers (n = 428)	UI Mothers (n = 141)
Personal		
Age, 1978 (years)	33.2	32.1
	(7.8)	(8.9)
Educational level, 1978	2.49[a]	3.00
	(1.02)	(1.02)
1 = 1 to 8 years	15%	6%
2 = 9 to 11 years	42%	29%
3 = 12 years	26%	30%
4 = 13 to 15 years	13%	29%
5 = 16 or more years	4%	6%
	100%	100%
Poor health, 1978	1.63	1.45
	(0.65)	(0.58)
1 = good health	47%	59%
2 = average health	43%	37%
3 = poor health	10%	4%
	100%	100%
Race (proportion white)	0.40	0.26
City (proportion Chicago)	0.54	0.45
Family		
Total number of children, 1978	2.4[a]	2.0
	(1.4)	(1.3)
Work and Income Support		
Previous job status [the first digit of the National Opinion Research Center ratings for job status ranging from 1 to 8—low to high—for those who ever worked]	2.6 (0.9) [370][b]	3.1 (1.1)
Previous job pay, 1973–1978 ($/week) [only those who worked at all during that time]	108[a] (50) [231][b]	148 (59)
Job pay of those working at time of 1979 reinterview ($/week)	118[a] (48) [121][b]	141 (53) [66][b]
Months on welfare, 1973–1978	37.6[a] (24.7)	10.2 (19.2)
Others' earnings in household, 1979 ($/week)	20[a] (64)	53 (113)
Economic independence through work, 1979	0.71[a] (1.12)	1.87 (1.26)
0 = Yes income support, No work	65%	27%
1 = Yes income support, Yes work	14%	5%
2 = No income support, No work	5%	22%
3 = No income support, Yes work	16%	46%
	100%	100%
Federal Intervention		
Proportion who got job through WIN	0.09 (0.28)	—

[a]The rating of WIN mothers is significantly different from the rating of UI mothers at the 0.01 level of probability or less.

[b]The number of respondents for this variable is in the square brackets.

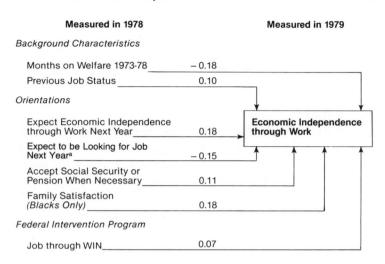

Measured in 1978   **Measured in 1979**

Background Characteristics

Months on Welfare 1973-78 _____ −0.18

Previous Job Status _____ 0.10

Orientations

Expect Economic Independence
through Work Next Year _____ 0.18

Expect to be Looking for Job
Next Year[a] _____ −0.15

Accept Social Security or
Pension When Necessary _____ 0.11

Family Satisfaction
(Blacks Only) _____ 0.18

Federal Intervention Program

Job through WIN _____ 0.07

**Economic Independence
through Work**

Note: For a detailed presentation of the regression equation upon which this figure is based, see table 3A−1.

The numbers associated with the arrows in all the figures are called "beta weights." They indicate the relative importance of the predictor variables. A beta weight of −0.18 connecting months on welfare to economic independence indicates that for a one unit rise in months on welfare, economic independence would *decrease* by 0.18 units.

The number of respondents given in each figure is the number for whom values of the dependent variable are available.

[a]This predictor consists of a single item. The item also appears with two other items in making up the WIN fathers' expectation of economic independence through work (see table 2−1).

Figure 3–1. Predictors of Economic Independence for 417 WIN Mothers

nomic independence. Key results are presented in figure 3–1. The arrows going from the independent variables measured in 1978 to the dependent variable measured in 1979 imply casualty. The relative impact of each independent variable is indicated by its beta weight shown in the figure. The complete statistical model, including control variables, is presented and explained in table 3A–1 in the appendix to this chapter.

One of the major findings of figure 3–1 is that none of the orientations measuring preference for welfare or UI (see table 2–1) are direct predictors of economic independence. Mothers who have a high preference for welfare are no more likely to have remained on welfare than mothers with a low preference. Other considerations are much more powerful than such preferences with respect to achieving economic independence. What are the other considerations? They include the four psychological orientations and two background characteristics listed in figure 3–1.

Expectations

One of the strongest predictors of economic independence is the expectation of achieving such independence (orientation 1, table 2–1). This finding confirms our hypothesis in chapter 2 about the relevance of expectations in guiding actions. The expectation of a mother in 1978 does more than reflect her own reaction to her background characteristics. If the expectation were no more than that, it would be displaced in the regression analysis by measures of background characteristics. The expectation carries psychological meaning over and above the background characteristics that might be associated with it.

Given the importance of this expectation of economic independence, the question arises as to how it might be influenced. In particular, how can it be raised among low-income persons? An answer is provided by considering the predictors of the expectation as it was remeasured during the 1979 reinterview.

Predicting the Expectation of Economic Independence. Figure 3–2 shows how the expectation of economic independence in 1979 is strongly affected by the expectation measured in 1978 and by the level of economic independence achieved in 1979. One of the most important findings of this study is the feedback relationship between *expectation* of economic independence and *achievement* of economic independence. WIN mothers who had higher expectations in 1978 tended to have higher levels of economic independence in 1979, even as those same mothers tended to raise their 1979 expectations of independence for the following year. The reverse side of the coin is that lower expectations lead to lower levels of economic independence, which, in turn, lead to lower expectations for the following year.

The feedback relationship between expectation and experience can cycle upward toward higher levels of expectation and achievement or downward toward lower levels of expectation and increased dependency on welfare. After a time such cycles are likely to reach some equilibrium, with a balance struck between expectation and experience. That is, life tends to settle into a pattern.

However, any such equilibrium is not fixed in concrete. The equilibrium is being maintained continuously through the experiences and interpretations of the persons involved. By the same token, the equilibrium can be altered in the course of having new experiences or new thoughts.

New opportunities provided through programs of training or job creation can lead poor persons to new experiences and higher expectations that may lead to a new equilibrium at a higher level of economic inde-

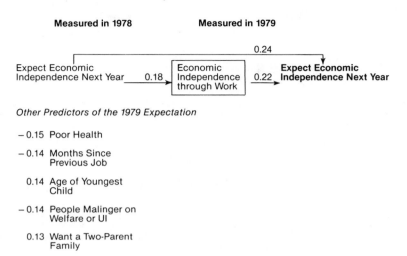

Other Predictors of the 1979 Expectation

  −0.15 Poor Health

  −0.14 Months Since
             Previous Job

    0.14 Age of Youngest
             Child

  −0.14 People Malinger on
             Welfare or UI

    0.13 Want a Two-Parent
             Family

Note: This figure combines the results of two regression equations. The first equation, illustrated in figure 3–1 and presented in detail in table 3A–1, provides the beta weight associated with the arrow leading from the 1978 expectation to economic independence through work—0.18. The second equation, in which the 1979 expectation is the dependent variable, provides all the other information. The beta weights precede the name of the predictors listed down the left side.

In this second equation, economic independence through work appears as an independent variable, whereas it was the dependent variable in the first equation. A feedback relationship is observed between expectation and achievement which probably operates continuously over time. The two equations describing the feedback process are interdependent because economic independence appears in both. It is appropriate in this situation to use a two-stage least-squares technique for estimating the 1979 expectation. This is accomplished by using in the second equation (which predicts the 1979 expectation) the values of economic independence that were estimated from the first equation rather than the empirical values of economic independence. The control variables used in the second equation are the same as those used in the first.

The total variance (R^2) of the 1979 expectation explained by all the predictors in the second equation is 0.34. (Further details regarding this equation are available from the author upon request.)

Figure 3–2. Predictors of the 1979 Expectation of Economic Independence for 404 WIN Mothers

pendence. New failures can lead in the opposite direction. The following conversation from a group interview illustrates the psychological reality of the downward cycle.

Mary: I've been on and off jobs so often I have to wonder if I got the job simply because the employer was forced to have someone from the WIN program.

Social scientist: No. There's no way to force anybody to hire anybody.

Mary: Because if I'm doing my job and I'm doing it prop-
                 erly, then why is it that six or eight months later I
                 don't have a job?

Olivia: Do you get fired or . . .

Mary: No, I don't get fired, just get laid off. I've got a long
                 list of laid offs, and I worked just as hard as anybody
                 else. So I've always wanted to know, does the gov-
                 ernment force these people to hire inexperienced
                 people?

Social scientist: They don't have any way of forcing that.

Mary: If they think they are doing us a favor, they're hurting
                 us more so. Because if you tell a person that they
                 have a job and everything inside of them is all excited
                 and prepared to go to work, and then when they go
                 to work they find out six months later they don't have
                 a job, and there's no valid reason as to why, they go
                 right back into the cycle. That's where it's unfair.

Mary's comment poignantly illustrates the psychological debilitation
that comes with expecting to continue in a job only to find the job
withdrawn. Mary did not let her negative experiences affect her own job
efforts. She was working part time as a security guard at the time of the
group interview. But one can understand how continued failure to maintain employment can erode many persons' expectations and efforts. Success would have the opposite effect.

While success in the work world may be the single most powerful
way of raising the expectation of economic independence, what other
ways exist? Figure 3–2 indicates that the expectation goes up as mothers
have been more recently employed. The importance of work affecting
expectation again is provided.

The expectation also rises as a mother's health improves and as her
children grow older. Provision of adequate health services can be a positive factor in raising expectations. Ages of children are not open to
artificial alteration. (If mothers have additional children, of course, the
age of their youngest child goes down. The psychological and social
issues of childbearing are beyond the scope of the present enquiry.)

It is understandable that some welfare mothers with very young children will hesitate to work the number of hours necessary to achieve
economic independence. It may be less obvious that mothers in the ghetto
feel the need to be home to protect their somewhat older children. The
following comment during a group interview illustrates the child-care
and health issues:

Lorraine: When I had to go to the hospital it was a thing for me to lay up there and worry about my kids because I know that in the project you are not safe. You are absolutely not safe.

I wasn't there four months before one of the little guys grabbed my [12-year-old] daughter on the elevator and he wanted her to talk to him. She wouldn't talk to him and he twisted her arm.

So I called the police, and the whole family was involved and I went to court. Just like I told the judge, and I meant this: "I come down here and I'm asking for help and begging for help. I am not telling her who to pick to talk to. But if she doesn't wish to talk to someone, he has no right to force her."

Single-parent mothers in poor urban neighborhoods have problems in protecting their children and their apartments. Several mothers pointed out during group interviews that households with men in them are not subject to as many robberies as households without men. The family demands on single-parent mothers also slow the recovery process from health problems.

Two orientations predict the 1979 expectation of economic independence. The more that mothers want a two-parent family, the higher their expectation. At first glance the result is paradoxical. Why should mothers who hold the goal of having a husband who supports the family tend to achieve higher levels of economic independence on their own?

There are two parts to the resolution of the paradox. First, if one considers the items that comprise the goal of a two-parent family (table 2–1), no item states the desirability of a mother staying home full time to look after her family. Such an item was included in the questionnaire, but it did not cluster with the items forming the orientation under consideration. Mothers are no longer viewing their role as full-time housekeepers. The group interviews indicate that many welfare mothers want a reliable husband even though they expect to work. This point is made by Donna in her perceptive remark about the changing family roles of men and women:

Donna: You see, the stereotype used to be the man had to work to provide for the family and the woman handled all the problems in the family. But it's changed now because now the women have to get out there and work too. So I think the time is coming where the man is going to have to share some of that responsibility of bringing up the children.

The second reason why mothers who want a two-parent family also expect to go to work and leave welfare stems from the isolating effect of welfare. There is little chance of meeting desirable men when staying at home; chances are better when one is out at work meeting people. This point will be amplified shortly in our discussion of why mothers stay on welfare. The point to emphasize here is that the goal of a two-parent family not only is strong among welfare mothers (a rating of 3.67 for "want a two-parent family"; orientation 19 in table 2–1), but indirectly influences mothers to move toward economic independence through raising their expectation of independence.

The final predictor of the 1979 expectation is the belief that people malinger on welfare and UI. High scores on this orientation probably reflect the respondent's own tendency to malinger. That is, persons tend to attribute their own persuasions to others. The fact that high scores on this orientation lead to lower expectation of economic independence suggests, therefore, that the expectation is partially influenced by an unwillingness to leave welfare. The impact of this orientation, however, is very small compared to the impact of all the other predictors that do not imply malingering on welfare.

We conclude that the expectation of economic independence is powerfully influenced by the kind of experience one has in the job market, is incidentally influenced by family considerations, and is very little associated with the idea of malingering on government support. The indirect impact of the malingering orientation on the actual achievement of economic independence, as mediated through the expectation of independence, is minute. When all the direct and indirect impacts of variables upon economic independence are taken into account, the effects of variables indicating preference for welfare or UI are negligible.[1]

Another Expectation

Another predictor of economic independence is the 1978 expectation of looking for a job next year (item 2c). The higher the rating on this expectation, the lower the level of achieved economic independence in 1979. This is reasonable in that a mother who has a high expectation of *looking* for work next year is indicating that she does not expect to be working at that time next year. How might this expectation be influenced to increase economic independence?

Consider the predictors of the 1979 measure of this expectation as seen in figure 3–3. One predictor is the 1978 expectation. The strongest predictor is the 1979 level of economic independence achieved. This makes eminent sense. As a mother experiences higher levels of achievement in the work world she will have more confidence in her ability to succeed in that world, thereby lowering her expectation of merely looking

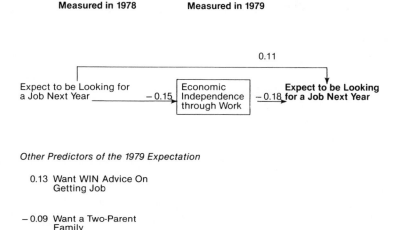

Figure 3–3. Predictors of the 1979 Expectation of Looking for a Job for 415 WIN Mothers

Note: For an explanation of the statistical analyses in this figure see the note for figure 3–2. The total variance (R^2) of the 1979 expectation explained by all the predictors is 0.08.

for work. Again, there is a feedback relationship between a psychological orientation and experience in the work world, and the strong impact of success or failure on the orientation.

The two orientations that also predict the 1979 expectation of looking for a job do not suggest malingering on welfare. The more that a mother wants a two-parent family, the less likely her expectation of merely looking for work. This is reasonable in the context of our earlier finding that mothers who wish to have a two-parent family tend to achieve economic independence. The second orientation reasonably indicates that those who want *advice* from WIN about getting a job, as distinct from wanting a job from WIN, tend to have higher expectations of merely looking for a job next year.

Acceptability of Social Security or Pension

The more that WIN mothers are willing to accept social security or a pension when necessary (orientation 12, table 2–1), the higher their achieved level of economic independence. These two kinds of income supports tend to accrue to middle-class workers. WIN mothers who find these supports attractive can be viewed as having middle-class aspirations. The way of achieving these supports is by working, because both are based on a considerable work history. Hence, it is reasonable that this orientation should predict achieved level of economic independence. We will consider the basis for this orientation's effectiveness again when the economic independence of UI mothers is discussed.

Family Satisfaction

The final orientation that predicts economic independence is family satisfaction (orientation 23, table 2–1). It is reasonable that level of satisfaction is positively related to achievement of economic independence. Mothers who feel their households are running well are more likely to feel free to go to work. Mothers who perceive family difficulties are less likely to leave the home when they are the sole head of household. This situation is illustrated in the following excerpt in which Chris talks of the difficulty of holding a fulltime job and also giving enough attention to her young child.

> Chris: I went through an experience with my little girl. I had to be at work at 9:30 and got home at 5:30. So I told her she is at an age where she can dress herself and fix her own breakfast, like a bowl of cereal or something like that.
>
> But by the time I got home in the evening, I'm running around that house trying to fix dinner, you know. And she'll be saying, Mama this and Mama that, and I'll say, "Wait baby, let Mama get through cooking. Mama'll get to you." About 9:00 I'm telling her to go to bed. I'm tired and I want her to go to bed.

Later in the group interview Chris mentioned that she quit her job and went back on welfare because of the combination of wanting more time to look after her daughter and the low wage that she was getting.

The puzzle in the statistical findings is why satisfaction with family functioning is predictive only for black WIN mothers and not for white WIN mothers. The predictors of that orientation (not shown here) are virtually the same for whites and blacks. The relationship between family functioning and work among black mothers is apparently different from that among white mothers. This difference should be elucidated in future studies. In any case, increasing family satisfaction among black WIN mothers—for example, perhaps by using social services to relieve certain child-care or other family problems—could lead to their increased achievement of economic independence.

Months on Welfare

The longer a mother has been on welfare during the 1973–1978 period, the less likely she is to achieve economic independence in 1979. This finding suggests the importance of mothers moving off welfare as quickly as possible if they are to avoid becoming trapped in that benefit program. Why have some mothers been on welfare longer than others? There are two rather different but equally plausible explanations. One is that mothers have strong preference for welfare and reject the idea of work. The other is that mothers do not have the background characteristics necessary for obtaining jobs that pay a living wage. Depending upon which explanation is correct, the implications for action are quite different.

Why Mothers Stay on Welfare

If mothers stay on welfare out of preference for that benefit program rather than economic necessity, the easiest way of moving them off welfare is to withdraw the benefits. However, if mothers are on welfare because of necessity, then there is reason to try to help them obtain adequate employment. To determine which explanation is correct, months on welfare from 1973 to 1978 can be made a dependent variable in a separate regression analysis.

The independent variables identified in this manner may not be causing time on welfare in a simple manner. Feedback processes may be at work. Identification of these processes is not crucial to our purpose. The important point is whether variables indicating preference for welfare are strongly associated with time on welfare.

When a regression analysis is conducted with months on welfare as the dependent variable, the primary independent variables turn out to be background characteristics.[2] By far the strongest predictor of months on welfare during the 1973–1978 period is the amount of pay mothers have been previously able to command in the job market. The lower the pay they command, the longer the time on welfare. Also, the lower their educational level and the more children they have, the longer the time on welfare.

Data from this study show that mothers do not stay on welfare because they prefer it or reject the idea of work. Not one of the seven orientations measuring preference for non-work income nor any of the orientations measuring normative beliefs about work in table 2–1 predict months on welfare. One orientation, however, does have a small effect on time on welfare. It is the expectation to receive welfare next year.

This orientation might be seen as signifying unwillingness to leave welfare and hence encouraging increased time on welfare. The reverse might also be true—time on welfare leads to a higher expectation of continuing on the program. It is likely that there is a feedback relationship between the orientation and welfare experience such as we have found between the expectation of economic independence and its achievement. The welfare experience may generate inertia to stay on welfare. This possibility is illuminated by the comments of two mothers during a group interview:

Betty: You find some people [on welfare] who are afraid of change and they get like in this rut. They're afraid to climb out of it. They're afraid to venture out.

Gert: That's the way I was on welfare. I wasn't working. I was home, I never went anywhere. I never met people. So finally after so many years when I got this job [school-crossing guard] I'm outside all the time. I meet people all the time, and I really feel like I am somebody now.

These comments illustrate how the welfare experience can keep one in the rut of welfare. They also illustrate an issue not revealed in the statistical analysis: welfare isolates a mother from contact with others, and hence social opportunities. When a single-parent mother is home all the time with her children she is not exposed to situations that might lead to jobs or marriage. In addition, employers may hesitate to hire mothers who have been on welfare, adding to the negative effect that months on welfare has on achieving economic independence.

Our research findings demonstrate that the major reason mothers spend time on welfare is economic necessity, their inability to command a living wage in the job market. Another, but subsidiary, reason is that they tend to get into a welfare rut. Removing welfare benefits would counteract the inertia associated with the welfare experience, but it would condemn mothers and their families to less than subsistence living. Providing the opportunity for welfare mothers to earn higher salaries than they now can command should lessen the time spent on welfare.

Getting a Good Job

The other background predictor of economic independence is previous job status. Mothers with higher-status jobs in the past tend to become economically independent in 1979, while mothers with lower-status jobs tend to remain dependent. Job status is strongly related to job pay, but it contains additional elements as well. Higher-status jobs—such as office work as compared with waitressing—tend to carry greater stability and job benefits. The following excerpt from a group discussion illustrates the importance of the benefits that come with higher-status better-paying jobs:

Betty: If you have a high paying job, probably there are going to be benefits like sick days.

Flo: And hospitalization.

Betty: Yes, and holidays and stuff like that, where you can get little things done.

Edith: Higher paying jobs have more benefits than lower paying jobs.

Ann: You need those things. Those are very important. You have to have those things.

Flo: The only reason I continue to stay on Aid, for the small amount I am allowed, is not so much for the money, but they give you the green card, the medical card. With waitressing, there is no insurance or anything where I am at.

         I don't know what I'd do if I had to pay hospitalization for any of my children. But this way I've got that security at this point until I can better myself, which I'm trying to do. I'd like to get off. I don't like it. But I'm going to hang in there with the medical card until I do better.

One can appreciate how a higher-status job improves a mother's ability to achieve full economic independence. Flo's comments about her waitressing job indicates how a low-status job, without benefits, encourages one to achieve only partial rather than full economic independence. The availability of fringe benefits (including social security and pension rights) in high-status jobs is probably a major reason why welfare mothers who qualify for such jobs move out of dependency.

The WIN Program

The WIN program has a positive impact on mothers' achievement of economic independence when it finds jobs for these mothers. The practical limitation of this finding is that WIN obtained jobs for only 9 percent of the mothers. (The others who obtained jobs said that they did not have WIN help.) The finding illustrates the same problem that beset WIN from its inception: inability to find enough jobs for welfare recipients. The poor performance of WIN is undoubtedly related to labor-market conditions.[3] The importance of such conditions will occupy our attention again.

Validity of Results

The validity of the results just presented is tested in various statistical ways in appendix D. It is useful, in addition, to compare the findings from welfare mothers with findings from other mothers who face a somewhat similar situation. An examination of why UI mothers achieve various levels of economic independence will further illuminate the significance and validity of our findings for welfare mothers.

Predicting the Economic Independence of UI Mothers

The UI mothers chosen for this study, as indicated in chapter 2, came from family situations and social economic status as much like the WIN mothers as possible. UI mothers have greater employment potential than WIN mothers (table 3–1). At the same time, 18 percent of the UI mothers interviewed in 1978 said they were on welfare. It was decided to keep these mothers in the sample because there appeared to be continuing traffic between the UI and welfare programs among low-income female heads of households. (A total of 38 percent of the UI mothers had been on welfare at some time during the five-year period from 1973 to 1978.) However, to ensure that the model would apply only to UI mothers *not* on welfare, a control variable was used in the equation that indicated whether the mother was receiving welfare. Only 64 percent of the mothers applying for UI were actually eligible for the program (as determined in the 1979 reinterview). The others had to depend on their own resources.

At issue is how the bases for welfare mothers achieving economic independence compares with the bases for UI mothers. Are there reasonable similarities and differences, or do results from the UI mothers question the validity of the WIN model? The model of economic independence for UI mothers is shown in abbreviated form in figure 3–4. Two orientations and one background characteristic constitute the model.

Expectation of Independence

For UI mothers, as for WIN mothers, the expectation of economic independence (orientation 1, table 2–1) is a major predictor of the level of economic independence achieved in 1979. In addition, level of economic independence achieved predicts the 1979 expectation of independence for the following year (see figure 3–5).

The same feedback relationship between expectation of independence and achievement of independence is observed among UI mothers as among

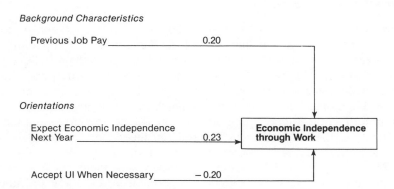

Note: For a detailed presentation of the regression equation upon which this figure is based, see table 3A–2. The numbers associated with the arrows are the beta weights.

Figure 3–4. Predictors of Economic Independence for 140 UI Mothers

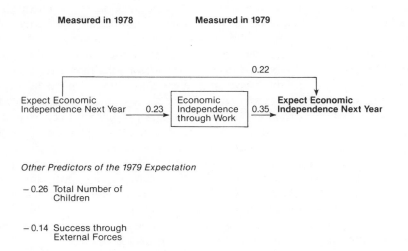

Note: For an explanation of the statistical analyses in this figure, but to be applied to UI rather than WIN mothers, see the note for figure 3–2. The total variance (R^2) of the 1979 expectation explained by all the predictors is 0.28.

Figure 3–5. Predictors of the 1979 Expectation of Economic Independence for 136 UI Mothers

WIN mothers. This finding adds to our confidence in the validity of the WIN mothers results.

Accept UI When Necessary

There is one sharp difference between the UI and WIN mothers. A major predictor of economic independence for UI mothers is acceptability of UI (orientation 9, table 2–1). The more that these mothers believe that UI is an acceptable form of income, the less likely are they to achieve a high level of economic independence. This finding suggests a tendency among UI mothers to remain dependent because of acceptance of the idea of an income-support program. It is possible, of course, that the UI mothers who have this tendency to remain dependent are using the additional time to search for better jobs or to look after their families.

The tendency for UI mothers to remain dependent because of the acceptability of an income-support program does not show up among WIN mothers. Indeed, acceptability of UI plays the opposite role for WIN mothers, as seen when the variables predicting economic independence for UI mothers are used to predict economic independence for WIN mothers (see table 3A–3 in the appendix to this chapter).

The higher the acceptability of UI for WIN mothers, the greater the achievement of economic independence. We interpret this finding to mean that WIN mothers' high acceptability of UI represents an aspiration for better jobs than they are usually able to command. The better jobs (generally those held by middle-class persons) are covered by UI and have other fringe benefits that the WIN mothers mentioned in the group interview excerpts. WIN mothers who strive for jobs that offer benefits such as unemployment insurance achieve greater economic independence.

This argument is an extension of the one we made to explain why high scores of WIN mothers on the acceptability of social security/pension orientation led to high economic independence. Not only is the present argument similar, but the major predictor of acceptability of social security/pension is acceptability of UI.[4] We conclude that poor persons who show high acceptability of income-support programs used primarily by middle-class persons are evincing their aspirations for middle-class status through work. When middle-class persons show a high acceptability of a middle-class–dominated income-support program they may be evincing a tendency to malinger on that program.

Previous Job Pay

The only background characteristic that predicts economic independence for UI mothers is level of pay on their previous jobs. The higher the pay, the higher the level of achieved independence. Although previous job pay is not a direct predictor of economic independence for WIN mothers, it is a strong indirect predictor. Months on welfare, which predicts economic independence for WIN mothers, is strongly predicted by previous job pay.[5] It is reasonable to find that the more UI and WIN mothers are capable of earning, the more they achieve economic independence.

The findings from UI mothers tend to substantiate those obtained from WIN mothers. Where there is a sharp difference in results, it indicates the greater likelihood of UI mothers remaining on a benefit program because of acceptance of it.

Summary of Findings for WIN Mothers

Those WIN mothers who remain dependent are distinguished from those who achieve economic independence by lesser ability to command a suitable wage in the labor market and by certain social and psychological orientations. Those WIN mothers who have higher expectations of achieving economic independence do, in fact, exhibit higher levels of independence. Those mothers who only expect to be looking for a job next year (rather than having one) exhibit lower independence. A major factor affecting both these orientations is the experience of success or failure in the work world. There is a feedback cycle between certain orientations and experiences that moves a person upward toward economic independence or downward toward continuing dependence.

An additional orientation that affects the achievement of economic independence has to do with middle-class aspirations. Mothers who are more strongly oriented toward middle-class income supports—social security and pension from a job—are more likely to work their way off welfare. How such an orientation can be affected is not clear. The greater the family satisfaction among black WIN mothers, the greater their achievement of economic independence. Why family satisfaction does not operate in the same fashion for white WIN mothers is unclear.

None of the direct predictors of economic independence include those orientations which measure preference for welfare of UI. Very few indirect predictors of economic independence measure preference for welfare or UI. The impact of these indirect measures in relation to all the direct and indirect predictors of economic independence is miniscule.

Although virtually no evidence indicates that preference for welfare influences mothers to stay on welfare, the negative effects of the welfare experience must be mentioned. The experience tends to isolate the mother socially and create the expectation of staying on welfare. The longer a mother is on welfare, the less likely are her chances of achieving economic independence. The way to reduce time on welfare is to provide greater earning opportunities for these mothers or encourage the fathers of these families to stay in the household and earn money.

If WIN mothers had husbands who were helping to support the family and helping to care for the children, life would be considerably easier for them and the welfare rolls would be considerably smaller. Why are the men who fathered the children of WIN mothers not staying with and helping to support these families? The present study cannot answer that question directly because no attempt was made to interview that sample of fathers. Significant light is shed on the matter in chapters 4 and 5, however, by examining both the basis for WIN fathers achieving economic independence and the basis for their staying with or leaving their families.

Notes

1. The complete set of indirect predictors of economic independence of WIN mothers is in Leonard Goodwin, *The Impact of Federal Income Security Programs on Work Incentives and Marital Stability* (Worcester, Mass.: Worcester Polytechnic Institute, 1981), pp. 4–22. Of the total of thirty indirect predictors, three deal with preference for welfare. The impact of those three indirect predictors compared to the twenty-seven others and the six direct predictors is virtually zero.

2. The following variables, preceded by their beta weights, appear in the multiple-regression equation in which "months on welfare 1973–1978" is the dependent variable for WIN mothers:

Background Characteristics
   −0.41 Previous job pay
    0.10 Total number of children
   −0.08 Educational level

Orientation
    0.14 Expect to receive welfare next year (item 1b, table 2–1)

R^2 (adjusted) total = 0.28

Control variables are race, city, age of youngest child, total number of children, adults working part time, adults working full time, and marital status.

3. In the following study that compared the administrative effectiveness of WIN programs in different geographical locations, it was

necessary to control for labor-market conditions because those conditions affected placement rates of WIN persons. For example, in areas with higher wage levels, there were greater numbers of job entries and greater reductions in welfare expenditures. See John J. Mitchell et al., *Implementing Welfare-Employment Programs: An Institutional Analysis of the Work Incentive Program,* R & D Monograph 78 (Washington, D.C.: U.S. Department of Labor, Employment and Training Administration, 1980), p. 32.

4. The following variables, preceded by their beta weights, appear in the multiple regression equation in which acceptability of social security or pension is the dependent variable for WIN mothers.

Orientations

0.47 Accept UI when necessary (orientation 9, table 2–1)

−0.11 Welfare preferred to work (orientation 5)

−0.08 Father should leave family if he cannot support them (orientation 15)

R^2 (adjusted) total = 0.25

Control variables are the same as those presented in note 2.

5. See note 2.

Appendix 3A
Complete Models
of Economic
Independence for
WIN and UI Mothers

Tables 3A–1 and 3A–2 contain both ordinary least-squares (OLS) models and tobit models of economic independence for the WIN mothers and the UI mothers. This dual analysis is carried out because the distribution of the dependent variable, economic independence, is peculiar in that there are many zero scores—many mothers who remain completely dependent on welfare (or UI) in 1979. That distribution is better represented by the tobit curve, a modification of the S-shaped probit curve, rather than the straight line of the OLS analysis. (For a discussion of tobit analysis, see James Tobin, "Estimation of Relationships for Limited Dependent Variables", *Econometrica* 26 (1958), 24–36; for a discussion of probit analysis, see D. J. Finney, *Probit Analysis,* 2nd ed., London: Cambridge University Press, 1962.)

The disadvantage of the tobit and probit analysis is that the departure from a straight-line representation removes any ready interpretation of beta weights and R^2. To obtain the greater explanatory use of OLS while avoiding the inclusion of possibly insignificant predictor variables in the models, the following procedure was used. An independent variable was included in the final model only if its coefficient was statistically significant at the 0.10 level of probability, a t value of 1.64 or greater, in both the OLS and the tobit analyses. For further discussion of the validity of the models presented here, see appendix D

Table 3A–1
Predicting Economic Independence for 417 WIN Mothers Who Head Households by Tobit and Ordinary Least-Squares Analyses[a]

Dependent Variable and Significant Predictor Variables	Tobit Means on Variables for Respondents		t Ratio for Regression Coefficient[b]		OLS	
	ECOI score = 0 (n = 272)	ECOI score = 1, 2, or 3 (n = 145)	Tobit	OLS	Regression Coefficient	Beta Weight[c]
Dependent Variable (1979)						
ECOI Economic Independence through Work 1979	0.00	2.06	—	—	—	—
Background Characteristics (1978)						
Months On Welfare 1973–1978	41.6	30.7	−3.6	−3.9	−0.0082	−0.18
Previous Job Status[d]	2.0	2.6	2.2	2.1	0.091	0.10
Orientations (1978)						
1. Expect Economic Independence through Work Next Year—Female	2.69	3.10	3.6	3.8	0.27	0.18
2c. Expect to be Looking for Job Next Year	2.87	2.44	−3.2	−3.3	−0.16	−0.15
12. Accept Social Security/Pension when Necessary	2.53	2.75	3.2	2.5	0.17	0.11
23B. Family Satisfaction (Blacks Only)[e]	2.56	2.65	3.4	3.3	0.36	0.18
23R. Interaction between Family Satisfaction and Race[e]	1.09	1.06	−3.4	−2.5	−0.45	−0.54
WIN Job (1978–1979)						
Got Job through WIN 1978 (proportion yes)	0.05	0.14	2.4	1.7	0.30	0.07
Controls[f]						
Race[e] (proportion white)	0.40	0.41	3.2	2.3	1.12	0.49
City (proportion Chicago)	0.55	0.48	−0.02	−0.2	−0.023	−0.01

Others' Earnings in Household, 1979 ($/week)	10	39	2.9	3.7	0.0031	0.18
Total Number of Children, 1979	2.4	2.3	-0.5	-0.9	-0.036	-0.04
Age of Youngest Child, 1979	8.0	8.2	-0.2	-0.4	-0.0059	-0.02
Marital Status, 1979 (proportion not living with mate)	0.93	0.83	-1.3	-1.6	-0.29	-0.08
Constant Term					-0.53	
Probability of ECOI = 0 (staying on welfare and not working) for WIN mothers giving the same scores to predictor variables that were given by WIN mothers who were on welfare and not working (who had zero scores for ECOI) in the present sample (see column 1 for mean scores)[g]			0.72			
Probability of ECOI = 0 (staying on welfare and not working) for WIN mothers giving the same scores to predictor variables that were given by WIN mothers who were either working and/or off welfare (had scores greater than "0" for ECOI) in the present sample (see column 2 for those values)[g]				0.51		
R^2 (adjusted) Background Characteristics[h]			0.10			
R^2 (adjusted) Orientations[h]			0.10			
R^2 (adjusted) Getting Job through WIN[h]			0.002			
R^2 (adjusted) Total[h]			0.20			

[a]The Tobit and OLS analyses were carried out on the INSTAT computer program developed by Dr. Joseph Tu while he was at Brookings Institution, Washington, D.C.

[b]Predictor variables are considered to be significant if they exhibit t ratios in both the OLS and Tobit analysis that are 1.64 or greater (see columns 3 and 4) indicating a probability of 0.10 or less of these variables having no predictive effect.

[c]The beta weights are useful in indicating the relative importance of the predictive variables in explaining the dependent variable. Each weight is determined by multiplying the regression coefficient by the ratio of the standard deviation of the predictor variable divided by the standard deviation of the dependent variable.

[d]The 58 mothers who never worked were given a status rating of zero.

[e]Satisfaction with family functioning (orientation 23, table 2–1) was found to be a significant predictor of economic independence for black WIN mothers, while not a significant predictor for white WIN mothers. To maintain this finding without splitting the WIN mothers into separate black and white groups (each of which would have substantially smaller numbers than the total group), Race was introduced as a dummy variable in two senses: a "slope dummy variable," 23R was created which consisted of the interaction of Race and orientation 23, in particular the product of orientation 23 scores and Race; and an "intercept dummy variable," Race itself (0 = black and 1 = white) was introduced. When these two variables, along with the regular value of orientation 23, are entered into the regression equation one obtains the following results:

1. The regression coefficient for orientation 23B now represents the value that would be obtained if one used the black group alone.

Table 3A–1 *Continued*

2. The regression coefficient of the interaction variable, orientation 23R, represents the extent to which orientation 23 is a better predictor of economic independence for black women than white women. The fact that the *t* ratio for orientation 23R is statistically significant indicates that it is legitimate to utilize the interaction variable in the equation.

3. The coefficient for Race represents the extent to which the constant term in the regression equation is changed as part of introducing the interaction variable. The coefficient for the Race term is statistically significant and positive, which indicates that whites have a greater level of economic achievement than blacks when Family Satisfaction is introduced as an interaction variable.

["Control variables" need to be taken into account in predicting the achievement of economic independence, but they either are not predictors of that achievement or else their effects need to be removed from the prediction. For example, a person can achieve a certain level of economic independence in 1979 because others in the household earn considerable money. Others' earnings is not a predictor variable because it was not measured until 1979, but we control for it to predict only that level of economic independence that is related to respondents' own characteristics.

City can be regarded as a predictor of economic independence since it has an effect in 1978. Our interest, however, is to discover characteristics that are effective predictors over and above one's city of residence. Hence, we introduce this variable into the equation whether or not it is statistically significant to control for it.

Control variables in a regression equation have beta weights and associated *t* values just as the predictor variables have. Thus, others' earnings in the household has a significant *t* value whereas City does not.

[The probability estimates made from the tobit analysis are not adjusted for degrees of freedom nor can the contribution of certain predictors be distinguished from others. Inclusion of the control variables in the tobit equation enhances the probability estimates. The probabilities presented in the table are obtained when only the predictor variables, and not the control variables, are included in the equation.

[In an OLS stepwise multiple-regression equation, the variables that are entered first tend to explain more variance (R^2) than if they are entered later. By entering the control variables measured in 1978 (Race and City) before the predictor variables, we are making sure that the predictors are not preempting variance that would be accounted for by the controls. (The controls measured in 1979, such as Others' Earnings or Total Number of Children were not entered before the predictor variables because they could not be considered predictors. It was possible for the 1978 versions of the 1979 control variables—for example, Total Number of Children in 1978—to have entered the regression equation as predictor variables. The fact that they did not indicates that they were not statistically significant.)

By entering background characteristics in the regression equation before the orientations, we are giving the former the maximum possible amount of explanation and correspondingly are giving the orientations a minimum amount. This is done to show that orientations are influential predictors of action over and above the effect of background characteristics. The amount of variance explained by obtaining jobs through WIN is obtained by entering that variable in the stepwise multiple-regression equation after the 1978 controls, background characteristics, and the orientations have been entered. The total variance (R^2) explained consists of adding together only the variance explained by background characteristics and the orientations.

Table 3A–2
Predicting Economic Independence for 140 UI Mothers' Households by Tobit and Ordinary Least-Squares Analyses[a]

Dependent Variable and Significant Predictor Variables	Tobit Means on Variables for Respondents		t Ratio for Regression Coefficient		OLS	
	ECOI score = 0 (n = 38)	ECOI score = 1, 2, or 3 (n = 102)	Tobit	OLS	Regression Coefficient	Beta Weight
Dependent Variable (1979)						
ECOI Economic Independence through Work	0.00	2.56	—	—	—	—
Background Characteristic (1978)						
Previous Job Pay ($/week)	131	157	2.5	2.6	0.0045	0.20
Orientations (1978)						
1. Expect Economic Independence through Work Next Year, 1979— Female	2.97	3.47	3.1	2.7	0.49	0.23
9. Accept UI when Necessary	2.97	2.77	-2.7	-2.6	-0.31	-0.20
Controls						
Race (proportion white)	0.18	0.27	0.6	1.0	0.22	0.08
City (proportion Chicago)	0.61	0.51	-0.3	-0.2	-0.03	-0.01
Proportion on Welfare, 1978	0.47	0.08	-3.6	-3.2	-0.88	-0.27
Proportion Received UI, 1978	0.57	0.67	0.3	0.5	0.09	0.04
Age of Youngest Child, 1979	6.7	7.1	0.7	1.0	0.017	0.07
Total Number of Children, 1979	2.2	1.9	-0.3	-0.7	-0.051	-0.06

Table 3A–2 *Continued*

Dependent Variable and Significant Predictor Variables	Tobit Means on Variables for Respondents		t Ratio for Regression Coefficient		OLS	
	ECOI score = 0 (n = 38)	*ECOI score = 1, 2, or 3 (n = 102)*	*Tobit*	*OLS*	*Regression Coefficient*	*Beta Weight*
Marital Status, 1979 (proportion not living with mate)	1.0	0.79	−2.8	−2.5	−0.74	−0.21
Others' Earnings in Household, 1979 ($/week)	33	57	1.4	1.3	0.0013	0.12
					1.17	
Constant Term						
Probability of ECOI = 0 for mothers with 0 scores	0.24					
Probability of ECOI = 0 for mothers with 1, 2, or 3 scores	0.10					
R^2 (adjusted) Background Characteristics						0.02
R^2 (adjusted) Orientations						0.08
R^2 (adjusted) Total						0.10

[a]See table 3A–1, notes.

Table 3A–3
Applying the UI Mothers' Economic-Independence Model to WIN Mothers

	WIN Mothers
Dependent Variable and Significant Predictor Variables	UI Mothers' Model t ratio (beta weight) (N = 417)
Dependent Variable (1979) ECOI Economic Independence Through Work	—
Background Characteristic (1978) Previous Job Pay	3.4[a] (0.16)
Orientations (1978) 1. Expect Economic Independence Through Work Next Year	4.5[a] (0.23)
9. Accept UI When Necessary	1.9[a] (0.09)
Controls Race (proportion white)	0.3 (0.01)
City (proportion Chicago)	0.1 (0.01)
Age of Youngest Child, 1979	−0.5 (−0.02)
Total Number of Children, 1979	−1.6[a] (−0.08)
Marital Status, 1979	−2.1[a] (−0.11)
Others' Earnings in Household, 1979	4.1[a] (0.20)
Constant Term	−0.22
R^2 (adjusted, not counting controls) Total	0.11

[a]t ratio significant at the 0.10 level of probability or less.

4

Causes of Fathers' Economic Independence

Providing welfare to fathers is not popular. This reluctance seems to stem from a fear that if poor fathers are offered an income option other than work, they will choose that option and avoid work. There are severe restrictions on the eligibility of fathers for welfare—for example, fathers cannot stay on welfare if they work more than 100 hours in a month regardless of the income they earn. Even then, only about half the states, primarily in the North, allow welfare for fathers. As a result of these and other reasons, only 5 percent of all AFDC recipients are fathers who head households.

Despite the small number of fathers on welfare, the factors that influence their achievement of economic independence are important to understand. That understanding can point the way to helping low-income fathers in general to reach economic independence. It is useful to begin by considering the background characteristics of WIN fathers in comparison with those of fathers applying for unemployment insurance.

Characteristics of the Fathers

Table 4–1 presents selected background characteristics of WIN and UI fathers. There is a distinct difference between these two groups of fathers: 54 percent of the WIN fathers did not graduate from high school, as compared with 31 percent of the UI fathers. Current weekly job pay (1979) among those working is $171 for WIN fathers and $212 for UI fathers. In addition, welfare households have less income from other family members and more children than the households of UI fathers.

The most striking difference between the WIN and UI fathers is the 1979 level of economic independence. Only 32 percent of the WIN fathers have achieved complete independence—are not receiving income support and are working—as compared with 77 percent of the UI fathers. Is this variation in economic achievement associated with different orientations toward UI or welfare?

Table 4–2 presents the mean values given selected orientations by the two groups of fathers. Expectation of economic independence is significantly higher for the UI as compared with the WIN fathers. This pattern is consistent with the variation in long-term work experiences

Table 4–1
Selected Characteristics of WIN and UI Fathers
(means or percent, standard deviations in parentheses)

Characteristics	WIN Fathers (n = 302)	UI Fathers (n = 141)
Personal		
Age, 1978 (years)	32.2	34.1
	(9.4)	(10.1)
Educational Level, 1978	2.62[a]	3.10
	(1.05)	(1.06)
1 = 1 to 8 years	12%	6%
2 = 9 to 11 years	41%	25%
3 = 12 years	24%	31%
4 = 13 to 15 years	18%	29%
5 = 16 or more years	5%	9%
	100%	100%
Poor Health, 1978	1.44	1.28
	(0.62)	(0.50)
1 = good health	63%	75%
2 = average health	30%	23%
3 = poor health	7%	2%
	100%	100%
Race (proportion white)	0.38	0.42
City (proportion Chicago)	0.50	0.48
Family		
Total Number of Children, 1978	2.4	2.1
	(1.4)	(1.2)
Marital Arrangement, 1978 (proportion living with mate but not married)	0.11	0.15
	(0.31)	(0.36)
Work and Income Support		
Previous Job Pay 1973–1978 ($/week) [only those who worked at all during that time]	168[a]	212
	(72)	(86)
	[279][b]	
Job Pay of Those Working at Time of 1979 Reinterview ($/week)	171[a]	212
	(76)	(82)
	[121][b]	[118]
Work Activity 1973–1978	3.33[a]	4.05
	(1.11)	(0.85)
1 = I never worked at all	8%	0%
2 = I worked less than half that time	18%	8%
3 = I worked about half that time	20%	10%
4 = I worked almost all that time	44%	51%
5 = I worked all that time	10%	31%
	100%	100%
Months on Welfare, 1973–1978	13	0.6
	(19)	(3.2)
Percent on Welfare, 1973–1978	57%	11%
Percent on UI, 1973–1978	52%	53%
Others' Earnings in Household, 1979 ($/week)	20[a]	82
	(58)	(145)
Economic Independence Through Work 1979	1.28[a]	2.71
	(1.33)	(0.60)
	[296][b]	

Table 4–1
Selected Characteristics of WIN and UI Fathers
(means or percent, standard deviations in parentheses)

Characteristics	WIN Fathers (n = 302)	UI Fathers (n = 141)
0 = Yes income support, No work	47%	2%
1 = Yes income support, Yes work	11%	1%
2 = No income support, No work	10%	20%
3 = No income support, Yes work	32%	77%
	100%	100%
Federal Intervention		
Proportion Who Got Job Through WIN	0.18 (0.38)	–

[a]The rating of WIN fathers is significantly different from the rating of UI fathers at the 0.01 level of probability or less.
[b]The number of respondents for this variable is in the square brackets.

Table 4–2
Selected Orientations of WIN and UI Fathers
(mean values, standard deviations in parentheses)

Orientations	WIN Fathers (n = 302)	UI Fathers (n = 168)
I. Expectations		
2. Expect Economic Independence through Work Next Year (measured in 1978)	3.02[a] (0.73)	3.31 (0.53)
2. Expect Economic Independence through Work Next Year (measured in 1979)	2.96[a] (0.71)	3.52 (0.49)
II. Preference for Nonwork Income		
4. Welfare is Good Way of Life	1.31[a] (0.71)	1.08 (0.35)
8. Accept Welfare When Necessary	2.32[a] (0.77)	1.78 (0.84)
10. Accept Government Support When Necessary	2.52[a] (0.65)	2.34 (0.63)
III. Normative Beliefs		
17. Family/Neighbors Look Down on Me for Receiving Welfare	2.21[a] (0.56)	2.38 (0.61)
IV. Family Relationships		
22. Want Others to Support Your Family	1.38[a] (0.47)	1.25 (0.40)
23. Family Satisfaction	2.83[a] (0.60)	3.02 (0.52)

[a]The rating of WIN fathers is significantly different from the rating of UI fathers at the 0.01 level of probability or less.

among the two sets of fathers—that is, UI fathers with a longer history of work activity during the 1973–1978 period can be expected to have higher expectations of working and being off an income-support program in 1979.

There is a consistent difference in mean values regarding preference for non-work income between the two sets of fathers. WIN fathers are more accepting than UI fathers of welfare and government support, although not of unemployment insurance in particular. WIN fathers see less disapproval from family and friends with respect to receiving welfare or UI than UI fathers. WIN fathers are also more willing to have others support their families than UI fathers. These findings can be interpreted in two ways: either as the result of WIN fathers having to resort to welfare to support their families or as an indicator of their continuing preference to have others support them rather than trying to achieve economic independence. The next step in the analysis tells us which of these explanations is correct.

Economic Independence of WIN Fathers

Our approach to developing a model of economic independence for WIN fathers is the same as that used for WIN mothers. That is, statistical techniques are used to determine the best predictors of economic independence from among all those predictors considered in the study. The WIN fathers' model of economic independence is presented in abbreviated form in figure 4—1. (The complete model appears in table 4A–1 in the appendix to this chapter.)

Similarities Between WIN Fathers and WIN Mothers

The WIN fathers' model, like that for the mothers, contains no orientations from among those measuring preference for welfare or UI. This suggests that WIN fathers' failure to achieve economic independence is not based on the attractiveness of government support. The fact that WIN fathers show relatively high acceptance of welfare in table 4–2 is an indicator of their past experience on welfare rather than an indicator of their unwillingness to try and get a job.

Expectation of Independence. A major similarity between the model for WIN fathers and WIN mothers is the strong predictive effect of the expectation to be economically independent next year (orientation 2, table 2–1). Moreover, the same feedback effect between this orientation

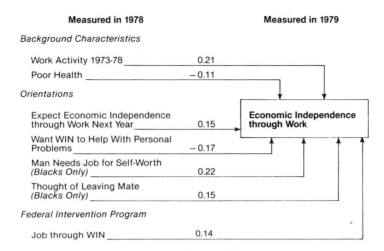

Figure 4–1. Predictors of Economic Independence for 296 WIN Fathers

Note: For a detailed presentation of the regression equation upon which this figure is based, see table 4A–1. The numbers associated with the arrows are the beta weights.

and achieved economic independence is noted in figure 4–2. Thus, WIN fathers as well as WIN and UI mothers exhibit the cycle in which expectations and experiences are strongly interrelated.

Comments from group interviews show that WIN fathers perceive this feedback relationship in their daily lives:

Carl: A lot of times a person that had some type of bad mental experience or something of that nature, a lot of times being disgusted, he doesn't have that motivation to be ambitious. He can get relaxed on welfare. He can also get relaxed on that job, just take it like it is, kind of overlook life.

In many cases a person is not just relaxed because he don't want to do better, but because he might not know how to do better, or because he got disgusted the time he did try to do better on a job. So through frustration it causes him to be relaxed.

He has tried and tried again and he has failed, and he has been unsuccessful. So it's not all the time the results of what happened. It's the cause. Once you get the chance, it is possible that he can be elevated to be able to want to improve himself in life.

These comments show that the statistical findings are not artifacts of our technical procedure but are portraying aspects of people's psychological reality. Failure in the work world erodes one's expectation of ever achieving independence and hence leads to lack of ambition.

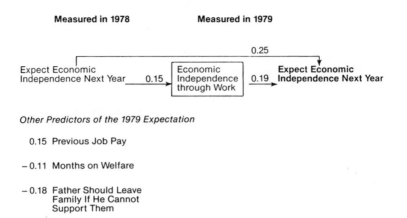

Other Predictors of the 1979 Expectation

  0.15 Previous Job Pay

 − 0.11 Months on Welfare

 − 0.18 Father Should Leave
         Family If He Cannot
         Support Them

Note: This figure combines the results of two regression equations. The first equation, illustrated in figure 4–1 and presented in detail in table 4A–1, provides the beta weight associated with the arrow leading from the 1978 expectation to economic independence through work. The second equation, in which the 1979 expectation is the dependent variable, provides all the other information. The beta weights precede the name of the predictors listed down the left side.

In this second equation, economic independence through work appears as an independent variable, whereas it was the dependent variable in the first equation. A feedback relationship is observed between expectation and achievement that probably operates continuously over time. The two equations describing the feedback process are interdependent because economic independence appears in both. It is appropriate in this situation to use a two-stage least-squares technique for estimating the 1979 expectation. This is accomplished by using in the second equation (which predicts the 1979 expectation) the values of economic independence that were estimated from the first equation rather than the empirical values of economic independence. The control variables used in the second equation are the same as those used in the first.

The total variance (R^2) of the 1979 expectation explained by all the predictors in the second equation is 0.30. (Further details regarding this equation are available from the author upon request.)

Figure 4–2. Predictors of the 1979 Expectation of Economic Independence for 289 WIN Fathers

The WIN Program. Another point of similarity with the WIN mothers' model is the positive impact of receiving a job through WIN. For WIN fathers, that occurrence substantially increases the achieved level of economic independence. However, only 18 percent of the fathers got jobs through WIN. This percentage is small even though it is larger than the 9 percent of the mothers who got jobs through WIN.

Background Characteristics. At first glance the background characteristics affecting economic independence for the fathers look different from those for the mothers. The major predictor for the fathers is the extent of work activity during the 1973–1978 period; for the mothers, the major predictor was months on welfare during the same time. However, work activity from 1973–1978 for the fathers is strongly related to months on welfare.[1] This strong relationship is not surprising because the more a father is unemployed, the more he would need to seek welfare. Another way of interpreting the finding (preferred by George Gilder and Robert Carleson) is that availability of welfare combined with lack of family and work commitment among welfare fathers decreases their work activity.

We can pursue these alternative explanations by considering the predictors of months on welfare from 1973 to 1978. The predictors are primarily background characteristics: low pay in previous job, low educational level, and the presence of young children and many children in the family.[2] Thus, as with WIN mothers, the length of time WIN fathers stay on welfare has a great deal to do with their inability to find jobs at which they can support their families and very little to do with orientations toward work or welfare.

The characteristic of poor health understandably lowers the achievement of economic independence among WIN fathers. This characteristic was not a direct predictor for WIN mothers. The reason was not that poor health was unrelated to economic independence; there was a direct, negative correlation. However, the expectation of economic independence was strongly related to poor health and replaced the poor-health variable in the model predicting WIN mothers' economic independence. Poor health did appear as a predictor of the expectation of economic independence (see figure 3–2) and hence was an indirect predictor of economic independence for WIN mothers.

Overall, the background characteristics affecting the economic independence of WIN fathers are similar to those affecting the independence of WIN mothers. This finding is reasonable in that factors of low pay, large families, and time on welfare should affect both female and male heads of households with respect to obtaining jobs that lead to economic independence.

Three Additional Orientations for WIN Fathers

We might expect that the orientations affecting WIN mothers and WIN fathers would be somewhat different because of their different roles in the family, with the man expected to be the main breadwinner. We have seen that the expectation of economic independence is similar for the mothers and the fathers (although it must be kept in mind that the measure of expectation is itself slightly different for men and women; see table 2–1). The remaining three orientations predicting economic independence for the WIN fathers are different from those in the WIN mothers' model.

Want Personal Help from WIN. The more that WIN fathers desire personal counselling, sympathy, help with child care and transportation to a job—component items of the want-personal-help orientation (orientation 29, table 2–1)—the less likely are they to achieve economic independence. Expression of these needs might suggest that the person or the household is disorganized to the extent that it affects the work activity of the father. One might also regard this expression of need as an excuse for not working. To evaluate these alternative interpretations, it is useful to examine the predictors of wanting help from WIN.

Predictors of Wanting Help from WIN. Lack of child care availability and the perception of family problems are directly related to the extent to which WIN fathers want help from WIN.[3] It might seem strange that child care would be a problem with a mother at home. However, the mother may be having great difficulty in managing household affairs, and 17 percent of the fathers indicate lack of suitable child-care arrangements (see table 4–1). Difficulty with child care and having family problems suggests a legitimate basis for wanting help from WIN.

The third predictor suggests another matter. Wanting personal help because one prefers welfare to work could indicate malingering on welfare. The strength of this orientation is not as great as that of the other two predictors combined, as seen in the beta weights assigned to these variables. Hence, one could conclude that wanting help from WIN is more a matter of legitimate need than of looking for an excuse to avoid work. (Preferring welfare to work is only an indirect predictor of economic independence; its impact on economic independence is extremely small when all the direct and indirect predictors of that dependent variable are taken in account.)

Man Needs Job for Self-Worth. The self-worth orientation (orientation 14, table 2–1) is significant only for black WIN fathers. The more strongly blacks believe that a man's self-worth is bound up with work, the more likely are they to obtain work and move toward economic independence. The meaning of this finding seems clear. But why is this orientation a predictor of economic independence only for black men?

A plausible explanation is that black men are more marginal to the work force than white men. (The unemployment rate for black men over 20 years old in Chicago in 1978 was 15 percent; for white men, it was 3.8 percent. Among men who are very uncertain of being able to find a job at which they can earn a living, some probably withdraw their feeling of self-worth from the job-holding effort. When unemployment occurs again, they may be slower to try to achieve economic independence because they no longer regard unemployment as undermining their self-respect. In this situation, those black men who still strongly identify their self-worth with work make a relatively greater effort to achieve economic independence and, in fact, find greater success in achieving independence.

This interpretation is illuminated by the following comment of a black man in response to the social scientist's query during a group interview:

Social scientist:	What do you think of the statement that a man really can't think well of himself unless he has a job?
Harry:	I think that's wrong. You see there's a lot of men that don't have jobs that still think well of themselves. It's up to the individual. Just because you're not working does not make you less than a man. You can go to some of these places right now that are hiring. A man is hiring. He looks at you and he'll say, "I'm not hiring." He don't want to be bothered with you. You never saw this guy before. Another guy will come along right behind you and get the job. So the man is a fool to think less of himself because he's not working. You got to get out there and look for that job. That's all there is to it.

Harry is referring to the experience of blacks being refused jobs without good reason while others who are white get the jobs. Harry explains the need of keeping one's own self-respect under those conditions, which means not using a job as a major criterion of your worth. At the end of his comment, Harry emphasizes the need to continue to look for work. However, it is reasonable to believe that as men withdraw their feeling of self-respect from having a job they may lessen their effort to obtain work. There is probably an interplay between the long-term experiences of black men in the work world and their scores on this orientation measuring self-worth through work that is not illuminated by the statistical data presented.

Among men who are more sure about their role in the work force— that is, white fathers—feelings of self-worth are less significant in achieving economic independence. Other orientations are influencing such achievement, such as expectation of independence. This is not to say that those white WIN fathers who strongly believe that a man needs a job for self-worth are undisturbed by being out of work. (The disturbance leads to marital disruption as seen in chapter 5.) Rather, this kind of disturbance does not improve efforts at finding work. These fathers already are trying as hard as they can to find employment.

Thought of Leaving Mate. The last orientation that predicts economic independence, again, for black fathers only, measures the extent one has thought about leaving one's mate (orientation 25). High scores on this orientation indicate strain in the marital relationship. It is paradoxical that high marital strain should predict high levels of economic independence. One might expect a father who is thinking of leaving his mate to exert less, rather than more, effort in the job market. One might speculate, however, that among blacks, where the man's labor-force activity is more tenuous than among whites, marital relations hinge on the extent of the man's work activity. Thus, when a black WIN father finds his marital relationship suffering he might think of trying harder to get a job to lessen the strain in the family situation. Additional efforts at job-hunting lead to greater achievement of economic independence. This social psychological line of reasoning should be subjected to further test in other research studies.

Summary of Statistical Results for WIN Fathers

There is virtually no reason to believe that WIN fathers are economically dependent because they accept the idea of welfare. (As reported elsewhere, only three of twenty-five indirect predictors and none of the direct predictors of economic independence express preference for welfare, making the overall impact of the three orientations negligible.[4]) Dependency comes about in part from their inability to obtain jobs at which they can support their families. Low expectations of future employment and need for help with personal problems also depresses the achievement of independence. Expectations can be raised by positive experiences in the job market, and help with personal problems can be provided through appropriate social services. Such efforts could help increase WIN fathers' achievement of economic independence.

For black WIN fathers, an increased belief that work is bound up with their self-worth leads to greater achievement of economic independence. What events increase such a belief is not altogether clear from this study. As black fathers perceive the possibility of leaving their family because of marital discord, they make a greater effort to achieve economic independence so as to lower the discord. These statistical findings from WIN fathers are usefully compared with these fathers' comments about work and welfare in the group interviews.

WIN Fathers Talk of Work and Welfare

Social scientist: Do you think there are men who prefer to be on welfare rather than work?

Adam: Yes, fifty-fifty. I feel that way.

Bob: From my point of view, I don't see the fifty-fifty. I think most men, I say around about up to 30 years of age, I think they prefer to work, but they want a job that's paying some money.

They don't want $3.10 an hour, you know. They want a job making at least $5 or $6 an hour. I believe men would prefer to work. I think most men do have that kind of pride within themselves.

But women, no. There are a lot of women who prefer to be on welfare. But I think more men want to work, if they are going to make a decent salary; $3.10 an hour is not a salary. You might as well be on welfare.

Adam: They put you on a job making $3 an hour, you are not on a job. People on welfare is getting that much.

Chet: Check this out. I got off of welfare and went to a job, right! I was making as an apprentice, I was making $3.30. When I brought my bring-home pay, it was $115. I used to collect every two weeks off of the welfare, it was $191.80 and food stamps was $106.

I say "Yes, let me get off", because like I got numb because I wasn't doing nothing. I was just waiting for the check to come and blasé, blasé around, feed my kids, pay all the bills, what I could flim-flam in between.

I took a job because I wanted, you know, I still had an interest to better myself. I was just making $30 more actually in cash money than I was collecting from the welfare a month.

Now you could buy a loaf of bread, a steak, some potatoes, onions, milk, you know, sugar. That is $30.

Dan: For one day.

Chet: That's $30.

Dan: For one meal.

Chet: That's $30.

Eric:

What happened is that here in this society a professional has a very high salary. But what about, for example, if we were making Xerox copies all day. That kind of work is very, very hard. Or, for example, if we work cleaning floors, or painting, or doing other handiwork. It is very hard.

We're men and we get tired after seven hours a day working. And how much we win? How much we earn? A little quantity.

This is not just because we have families; we have our wives, our daughters, our sons. We have to support them and we work hard.

We spend a lot of energy working and our salary is very, very low. This is inhuman. This is unjust.

Now, there are jobs, for example, the WIN program is offering. You go to the WIN program, there is a lot of jobs there and the salary is very, very, very low. This is unjustice.

Adam:

I had been in training. After they found out my age, they told me that it wouldn't be official for me to take the training because I'm too old. I'm 46. By the time they train me, I'll be too old to be on the job. That's one of them things.

Nate:

You can't win for losing. [Laughter]

Bob:

WIN got me a job like cabinetmaker. The employer said they're going to give me $3 an hour to start. I was supposed to get a quarter here and a quarter there. I never got anything.

I never learned anything that I didn't already know, which I explained to them at the WIN program. I already knew about factory work because I had done this before.

I am up in my 30s in years of age. I have done this when I was 19 and 20 years old. I've done factory work before, power press operator, spot welding here and there. I worked with shear cutters and stuff like that.

But I thought maybe I ws going to advance in this kind of field, I'm going to learn something more. They never really taught me anything. What it turned out, the whole thing was for six months. Everybody got laid off and it closed down.

When it came time for me to file income tax, I went to like my lawyer—I used to go there years ago when I had a steady job. He told me it would be a waste of time for me to even file for this income tax because I didn't even receive a statement from this job.

	All I had was check stubs. And these check stubs were funny, with a deduction here and a deduction there. I didn't get nothing for the W-2 forms.
Social scientist:	The employer took money out from your check?
Bob:	He took the money out every week, but I never received nothing.
Social scientist:	Did you get another job after that?
Bob:	I had a job after that. I got it on my own. I have one right now on my own. It is not full time. It is like a part-time job. I work six hours a night.

The comments of these men indicate a readiness and willingness to work. But there are feelings of frustration when they do not earn enough to support their families above the welfare level. These men do compare their earnings with what they can get on welfare. The question is raised as to what constitutes a fair welfare payment. This issue will be discussed in chapter 7. It is also clear from the group interview comments that keen disappointment follows unfair practices of certain employers of low-skilled persons. Another way of gaining additional insight into the meaning of the factors affecting WIN fathers' achievement of economic independence is to examine the factors affecting UI fathers' achievement of independence.

Predicting the Economic Independence of UI Fathers

The UI fathers are substantially better off economically than the WIN fathers. Most striking of all, only 3 percent of the UI fathers were receiving income support at the time of reinterview as compared with 57 percent of the WIN fathers. This difference creates a statistical problem. With only 3 percent of the UI fathers receiving a zero or 1 score on economic independence, that measure ceases to be a meaningful dependent variable. The scores on economic independence are bunched up at the top end of the scale rather than being distributed across the scale.

Defining Average Economic Independence

Needed is a dependent variable that measures a similar concept to economic independence but has the scores spread over the entire range of the zero to 3 scale. Such a variable is the average economic independence, which is obtained by averaging the measures of economic independence for each month between interviews. These monthly values are obtainable from retrospective answers to questions asked in the 1979 reinterview (see the appendix to chapter 3). The new variable, average economic independence (ECIA), has an adequate distribution of scores and is a satisfactory dependent variable.

There is an additional problem. Of the men in the UI fathers category, 17 percent were rejected as participants in the UI program. Those fathers needed to find a job quickly to support their families. Most of them did find a job (only 2 out of 28 went on welfare). The average economic independence score of this group of fathers is quite high because of their high work effort in the period between the two interviews. The average economic independence score of the fathers receiving UI benefits is much lower, since the receipt of benefits means that they remained unemployed for a period of time (see table 4–1).

One would expect the predictors of average economic independence to be quite different for these two groups of fathers. The fathers who received benefits could afford to stay on the UI benefits if they did not find suitable employment. In such a situation, where there is a strong element of choice, orientations should play a significant role in determining the action taken. The fathers who failed to receive benefits were under pressure to obtain immediate employment. Their employment activities should be influenced greatly by background characteristics that affected their employability and family characteristics that affected their need for money.

Figure 4–3 presents the abbreviated average economic independence models for the 133 fathers who received UI benefits during the 1978–1979 period and the 28 fathers who did not receive benefits. (See table 4A–2 for complete models.) Our expectations are confirmed in that orientations dominate the average economic independence model for the fathers receiving UI whereas background characteristics comprise the entire model for the fathers not receiving UI.

Model for Fathers Receiving UI

Four orientations account for most of the explanation of the average economic independence of UI fathers who received benefits.

Liked Previous Job. The first orientation listed in figure 4–3 that predicts economic independence is how much one liked his previous job. (This orientation is made up of a single item rated on a four-point scale that asked "Overall, how much did you like that [previous] job?") It is

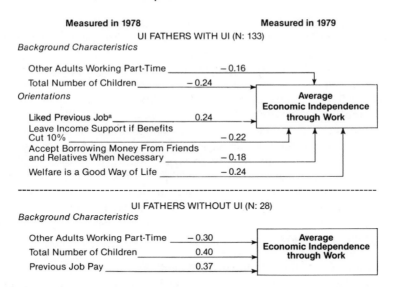

Note: For a detailed presentation of the regression equations upon which this figure is based, see table 4A–2. The numbers associated with the arrows are the beta weights.
[a]This orientation consists of a single item, "Overall how much did you like that job?" rated on a four-point scale that ranged from Not At All to Very Much.

Figure 4–3. Predictors of Average Economic Independence for 168 UI Fathers With and Without UI

reasonable to find that the more a father liked his job the more willing he is to go back to work and leave the UI program.

Intend to Leave Income Support if Benefits Cut 10%. It might seem paradoxical at first glance that the more UI fathers intend to leave income support if benefits are cut (orientation 3, table 2–1), the lower their average economic independence. One might think that fathers who are ready to leave income support when benefits decrease are those who feel they can earn more in the job market. There is, however, another way to view the situation, based on the characteristics of UI benefits.

UI recipients do not all receive the same amount of benefits. Benefits are based on previous earnings up to a maximum amount. In 1978, unemployed workers could receive about half the salary they earned during the previous year, up to a maximum of about $115 per week.[5] A father receiving the maximum benefits can better withstand a 10 percent cut, in terms of the absolute amount of dollars he receives, than a father receiving only half of the maximum amount. Moreover, the father receiving the higher benefit has better prospects of a higher-paying job in the future, inasmuch as he earned more in the past. He may be more willing to wait out a longer period of unemployment while looking for a higher-paying job than the father who has less prospect of obtaining a higher-paying job.

These speculations are supported by reviewing the predictors of the intention to leave income support if benefits are cut.[6] The strongest background predictor is household income. The higher the household income, the less the father is willing to leave income support if the benefits are cut 10 percent. The father who has other sources of income is willing to stay on UI even if benefits decrease; the father without those sources is more inclined to go immediately to work. The orientations predicting intention to leave if benefits are cut by 10 percent also suggest that fathers with more resources are more reluctant to leave the benefit program. This suggests the possibility of malingering on UI by fathers with more resources—that is, they continue on the program when they could find employment and leave.

Borrowing Money and Welfare is a Good Way of Life. These two orientations that predict average economic independence deal with alternatives to earned income. Father who find it more acceptable to borrow money from friends and relatives (orientation 11, table 2–1) achieve lower levels of average economic independence. This might result from their ability to borrow money successfully and therefore postpone reentry into the work force.

Those UI fathers who hold more strongly to the view that welfare is a good way of life (orientation 4) exhibit lower average economic independence. This suggests the possibility of malingering on UI—remaining on the benefit program because one finds it attractive to obtain income without work.

Background Characteristics. The two background characteristics predicting average economic independence provide additional insight into the UI fathers bases for action. The more these fathers have others in the household working part time, the lower the fathers' average economic independence. Apparently the fathers are less in a hurry to leave UI when they have another source of household income. The present data do not indicate whether the fathers use this additional time to search for better jobs or carry out other activities.

The greater the number of children in the household, the lower the fathers' achievement of average economic independence. One might expect the opposite to occur; that is, fathers with large families quickly finding work. However, because it is necessary to earn more to adequately support a large family, these fathers may take more time to find the best-paying jobs.

UI Fathers Who Did Not Receive UI

The model of average economic independence for the twenty-eight fathers who applied for but did not receive UI is seen in figure 4–3. All three predictors in the model are background characteristics, supporting the view that the orientations measured in this study become dominant only when there is a reasonable choice between working and not working. If these twenty-eight unemployed fathers were going to stay with their families, they had little choice except to find work as quickly as possible (or go on welfare, which they did not do).

Like the fathers who received UI, the fathers who did not receive UI were less likely to achieve high average economic independence if others in the household had part-time work. When it comes to the effect of having a large number of children, however, there is a reversal of results. Those fathers who failed to receive UI and had many children tend to exhibit high average economic independence. It is understandable that men with large families and no UI benefits will move quickly to earn money, whereas those who have benefits and large families may take longer to locate the best-paying job.

It is also reasonable to find that, among the twenty-eight fathers with no benefits, those who had higher earnings in the past achieved higher average economic independence during the 1978–1979 period. The fact that previous job pay is not a predictor for fathers who received UI suggests once again that higher-income recipients are staying on the program even though there are opportunities to obtain employment.

Comparing WIN and UI Fathers

The economic-independence model for WIN fathers is quite different from the average economic-independence model of either group of UI fathers. Considering the UI fathers who received UI, 1973–1978 work activity is not a significant predictor of their average economic independence, whereas such work was significant for the WIN fathers. Expectation of economic independence, which played an important role in the achievement of economic independence for WIN fathers, plays no role for UI fathers.

The UI fathers have a history of fairly consistent employment (their 1973–1978 work activity is listed in table 4–1). Their concern is not whether they can or should go to work, but what is the most suitable job for them. The average economic-independence model of UI fathers who receive UI is dominated by a concern for obtaining the best arrangement of income-support benefits relative to work, rather than a concern for finding work. If there is any hint of malingering on a benefit program, it is to be found among fathers who receive UI benefits.

The economic-independence model for WIN fathers, on the other hand, shows virtually no signs of malingering. It is dominated by orientations related to finding work and by background characteristics related to employability in the job market.

Explaining the Differences

A way of explaining the differences between the WIN and UI models is by reference to the different situations in which the two sets of fathers find themselves. If UI fathers were placed in the same uncertain and sporadic employment situation as the WIN fathers, one might argue that they would develop the same bases for action as the WIN fathers. One could also argue that WIN fathers would look like UI fathers if they had the UI fathers' job skills. Although these arguments appear to be valid, there are the deeper questions of how the fathers got into their different situations and how they might alter the situations.

It is here that our feedback model regarding attainment of economic independence is of special use. "Situations" are not rigidly fixed. The sporadic employment (and sporadic economic dependency) of WIN fathers results from the interplay among job market requirements, background, and family characteristics of the fathers, as well as orientations of the fathers (see figures 4–1 and 4–2). Changes in one or more of these factors can influence the situation.

Over time, however, it becomes more difficult for a person to initiate changes that will alter the employment situation. For example, as a man grows older and has to support a family, it becomes more difficult for him to upgrade his background characteristics to become eligible for higher-paying jobs. Hence, an equilibrium can be reached in which individuals' orientations, characteristics, and job experiences become mutually supportive of a low level of subsistence, including time on welfare.

Federal-intervention programs can help in altering the equilibrium in a positive fashion. One form of intervention that has been tried experimentally is a guaranteed income. The policy significance of such a guarantee will be mentioned in a moment. Of prior interest is the relationship of the experimental findings to findings just reported for the present study.

Critique of the Seattle-Denver Labor-Force Findings

The most extensive of the guaranteed-income experiments was conducted in Seattle and Denver. It compared the work activity of heads of families who received guaranteed payments when income fell below a certain level with the work activity of heads of families who did not receive such guaranteed payments. The latter families constituted the control group.

Of special concern is the purported finding that male heads of households lowered their labor-force activity as a result of the guarantee.[7] The Seattle-Denver researchers do not explain why this happened; they did not measure relevant psychological orientations; yet they implied that fathers in the experiment preferred income support to work. Such an implication runs counter to the findings in this study. WIN fathers do not lower their achievement of economic independence because of preference for income-support programs. The discrepancy in the two sets of findings may be resolved by examining more closely the conditions of the Seattle-Denver experiment.

The Flaw in Nonrandom Assignment

Persons were not assigned to the experimental or control groups in Seattle and Denver on a completely random basis. Lower-income families were purposely assigned in larger numbers to the experimental treatment while higher-income families were assigned in larger numbers to the control group. This was done so that the income guarantees would offer families realistic alternatives to work. If families assigned to the experiment normally earned high incomes, few would choose the relatively low-level income guarantee. The higher-income level of the control group was corrected for by taking into account income differences and other background characteristics in the statistical analysis.[8]

The statistical correction, however, may have been inadequate. Nonrandom assignment opens the possibility of differences between experimental and control groups that affect work activity but that are not measured and hence are not controlled in the statistical analysis. Our claim is that there very likely was a significant difference between the experimental and control groups.

The data reported in this book indicate that lower-income heads of households tend to have lower expectations of achieving economic independence than higher-income heads of households. Thus, when families with lower incomes predominate in the experimental group while families with higher incomes predominate in the control group, it is likely that the two groups also differ with respect to level of expectation of achieving economic independence.

This present study also shows that unemployed heads of households with low expectations exhibit lower achievement of economic indepen-

dence than those unemployed heads of households with high expectations. Hence unemployed members of the Seattle-Denver experimental
group would be less likely to return to work in a given period of time
than those in the control group because of their lower expectations of
achieving economic independence, not because they preferred the guaranteed income to work.

Consonant with our interpretation is the Seattle-Denver finding that
heads of families in the experimental group showed lower labor force
activity because they less readily reentered employment after being out
of work than heads of families in the control group. Heads of families
in the experiment left employment no more readily than heads of families
in the control group.[9] Our results suggest that the labor-force withdrawal
of fathers in the experimental groups might have been no greater than
those in the control group if the level of expectation of achieving economic independence had been the same in both groups. The dire warning
offered by Seattle-Denver experimenters to Congressional leaders—that
a guaranteed income would cost billions of extra dollars because a significant percentage of low-income heads of families would work less in
preference for the guaranteed income—might have been unwarranted.[10]
Moreover, by raising the expectations for economic independence of low-
income heads of families through appropriate job opportunities and other
steps predicated by our model of economic independence (see figure 3–
1), tendencies toward labor force withdrawal could be counteracted.

There is no way to determine whether our interpretation of the Seattle-
Denver results is correct (short of rerunning the experiment). Findings
reported in this book make it a reasonable possibility. These comments,
however, should not be interpreted as support for a guaranteed income
as a solution to the welfare situation.

Need for More Productive Policies

A guaranteed income is markedly limited with respect to helping the
poor who are not aged or disabled. Although it can help keep the poor
from starving, even as the welfare system plays that role, it does not
open up new opportunities. This point is emphasized by a WIN father,
George, in the group interview excerpted in chapter 6: "If you really
look at the welfare system today, it's not there to help us get any place.
It's to hold us in one place." Neither the welfare system nor a guaranteed
income provides large-scale job or training opportunities. Neither effort
is aimed at depleting the welfare population. To provide an adequate
basis for considering other intervention possibilities, it is important to

understand how unemployment and provision of government benefits affect marital relationships. The next chapter takes up that issue.

Notes

1. The following variables, preceded by their beta weights, appear in the multiple regression equation in which 1973–1978 work activity is the dependent variable for WIN fathers:

Background Characteristics
−0.40 Months on welfare 1973–1978
  0.35 Previous job pay

Orientations
  0.14 Expect economic independence next year (orientation 2)
  0.12 People Malinger on Welfare or UI (orientation 7)

R^2 (adjusted) total = 0.41

The control variables used in each regression equation reported in these notes were race, city, marital status, age of youngest child, total number of children, other adults working full time, other adults working part time.

2. The following variables, preceded by their beta weights, appear in the multiple-regression equation in which 1973–1978 months on welfare is the dependent variable for WIN fathers:

Background Characteristics
−0.16 Months on UI 1973–1978
  0.15 Age of youngest child
−0.14 Previous job pay
  0.13 Total number of children
−0.11 Educational level

Orientations
−0.18 Expect economic independence next year (orientation 2)
  0.12 Accept welfare when necessary (orientation 8)

R^2 (adjusted) total = 0.14

The variable "expect economic independence next year" predicts both 1973–1978 months on welfare and 1973–1978 work activity (see note 1). Although these activities occurred prior to the measurement of the orientation, there is probably a feedback effect between these activities and the orientation as elucidated in chapter 3 for the WIN mothers. This effect does not indicate malingering on welfare, but rather the way in which failure in the work force and the need to accept welfare depresses one's expectations of reaching economic independence. There is one other orientation predicting work activity—"accept welfare when necessary"—and one orientation predicting months on welfare—"people malinger on welfare or UI"—that might be construed as willingness to accept welfare rather than go to work. The relative impact of these orientations, as seen by the beta weights assigned to them in comparison with the sum of the weights assigned to other variables, is very small. The impact of these two orientations upon the level of economic independence achieved is virtually zero.

3. The following variables, preceded by their beta weights, appear in the multiple-regression equation in which "want WIN help with personal problems" (orientation 29, table 2–1) is the dependent variable for WIN fathers:

Background Characteristics
−0.20 availability of child care

Orientations
   0.20 Welfare preferred to work (orientation 5)
   0.13 Have family problems (orientation 24)

R^2 (adjusted) total = 0.10

4. Leonard Goodwin, *The Impact of Federal Income Security Program on Work Incentives and Marital Stability*. Worcester, Mass.: Worcester Polytechnic Institute, 1981, pp. 5–16.

5. In July 1978, the maximum UI benefits in Illinois ranged from $121 to $145 per week, depending on whether one had children or not. The flat maximum payment in New York State was $115 per week. See *Significant Provision of State Unemployment Insurance Laws, July 2, 1978* (Washington, D.C.: U.S. Department of Labor, Employment and Training Administration, Unemployment Insurance Services).

6. The predictors of the variable "intend to leave welfare or UI if payments cut 10 percent" (orientation 3, table 2–1) preceded by their beta weights, follow:

Background Characteristics
−0.20 Household income 1977
   0.15 Marital separation 1977–1978

Orientations
   0.28 Intend to leave welfare or UI for $100 a week job

0.19 UI helps family with money problems

R^2 (adjusted) total = 0.18

The first orientation consists of two items that are identical with respect to the initial statement, "If you could get a job paying $100 a week," but which are prefaced by two different statements: (1) "If you were on welfare, how likely would you be to go off"; and (2) "If you were receiving unemployment insurance, how likely would you be to go off." The two items were rated on a four-point scale that ranged from not at all likely to very likely.

The second orientation consists of a single item rated on a four-point scale from strongly disagree to strongly agree: "When I applied for unemployment insurance this time, I felt that getting unemployment insurance money would make things easier for my family."

7. Philip K. Robins and Richard W. West, "Labor Supply Response of Family Heads Over Time," in *A Guaranteed Annual Income,* ed. Philip Robins et al. (New York: Academic Press, 1980), pp. 85–99.

8. Ibid., p. 88.

9. Robert G. Spiegelman et al., "Additional Evidence on the Work Effort and Marital Stability Effects of the Seattle and Denver Income Maintenance Experiments," *Testimony before the Subcommittee on Public Assistance of the Senate Finance Committee, November 15, 1978* (Menlo Park, Calif.: SRI International 1978), p. 9.

10. Ibid., p. 9.

Appendix 4A
Complete Models
of Economic
Independence for
WIN and UI Fathers

Table 4A–1 contains both an ordinary least-squares (OLS) model and tobit model of economic independence for WIN fathers. The reason for this dual analysis and its use in determining the final model is presented in the appendix to chapter 3.

Table 4A–2 contains only an OLS model for each set of UI fathers—those who did and did not receive UI. The dependent variable in this case, average economic independence, has a normal distribution with very few zero scores.

Table 4A–1
Predicting Economic Independence for 296 WIN Fathers by Tobit and Ordinary Least-Squares Analyses[a]

Dependent Variable and Significant Predictor Variable	Tobit Means on Variables for Respondents		t Ratio for Regression Coefficient[b]		OLS	
	ECOI score = 0 (n = 137)	ECOI score = 1, 2, or 3 (n = 159)	Tobit	OLS	Regression Coefficient	Beta Weight[c]
Dependent Variable (1979)						
ECOI Economic Independence through Work	0.00	2.39	—	—	—	—
Background Characteristics (1978)						
Work Activity 1973–1978	2.91	3.69	4.3	3.7	0.25	0.21
Poor Health	1.60	1.30	−2.4	−2.0	−0.24	−0.11
Orientations (1978)						
2. Expect Economic Independence through Work Next Year	2.82	3.81	2.6	2.7	0.27	0.15
30. Want WIN Help with Personal Problems	2.50	2.24	−3.1	−3.1	−0.31	−0.17
14B. Man Needs Job for Self-Worth (Blacks Only)[d]	2.57	2.81	3.8	3.4	0.33	0.22
14R. Interaction between Man Needs Job for Self-Worth and Race[d]	0.91	1.16	−2.9	−2.8	−0.49	−0.51
26B. Thought of Leaving Mate (Blacks Only)[d]	1.77	1.86	2.4	2.2	0.24	0.15
26R. Interaction between Thought of Leaving Mate and Race[d]	0.68	0.75	−2.5	−2.6	−0.42	−0.34
Win Job (1978–1979)						
Got Job through WIN	0.11	0.24	3.0	2.7	0.48	0.14

Controls[e]						
Race (proportion white)[d]	0.34	0.43	3.8	3.9	2.21	0.81
City (proportion Chicago)	0.42	0.57	1.5	1.0	0.14	0.05
Others' Earnings in Household 1979 ($/week)	9	30	3.2	3.1	0.0037	0.16
Total Number of Children 1979	2.6	2.3	−0.4	−0.7	−0.035	−0.04
Age of Youngest Child 1979	NA[f]	NA	NA	0.8	0.015	0.05
Marital Status 1979 (proportion not living with a mate)						
Marital Arrangement 1979 (proportion living with mate but not married)	0.06	0.09	1.2	0.9	0.24	0.05
Constant Term	0.08	0.06	−1.1	−1.4	−0.40 / −1.01	−0.08

Probability of ECOI = 0 (staying on welfare and not working) for WIN fathers giving the same scores to predictor variables that were given by WIN fathers who were on welfare and not working (who had 0 scores for ECOI) in the present sample (see column 1 for mean scores) — 0.55

Probability of ECOI = 0 (staying on welfare and not working) for WIN fathers giving the same scores to predictor variables that were given by WIN fathers who were either working and/or off welfare (had scores greater than 0 for ECOI1) in the present sample (see column 2, for those values)[g] — 0.27

R^2 (adjusted) Background Characteristics[h] — 0.13
R^2 (adjusted) Orientations[h] — 0.08
R^2 (adjusted) Total[h] — 0.21
R^2 (adjusted) Getting Job through WIN[h] — 0.02

[a] The Tobit and OLS analyses were carried out on the INSTAT computer program developed by Dr. Joseph Tu while he was at Brookings Institution, Washington, D.C.

[b] Predictor variables are considered to be significant if they exhibit t ratios in both the OLS and Tobit analyses that are 1.64 or greater (see columns 3 and 4), indicating a probability of 0.10 or less of these variables having no predictive effect.

Table 4A–1 *Continued*

[c]Beta weights are useful in indicating the relative importance of the predictor variables in explaining the dependent variable. Each weight is determined by multiplying the regression coefficient by the ratio of the standard deviation of the predictor variable divided by the standard deviation of the dependent variable.

[d]See table 3A–1, note e, for a discussion of racial interaction variables.

[e]See table 3A–1, note f, for a discussion of control variables.

[f]Data are not applicable.

[g]The probability estimates made from the tobit analysis are not adjusted for degrees of freedom nor can the contribution of certain predictors be distinguished from others. Inclusion of the control variables in the tobit equation enhances the probability estimates. The probabilities presented in the table are obtained when only the predictor variables are included in the equation.

[h]The R^2 values have been obtained by entering race and city first in the stepwise multiple-regression equation, followed by the background characteristics, and finally by the orientations. This provides a minimum estimate of the effect of the orientations and a maximum estimate of the effects of the background characteristics Total R^2 is the effect of background characteristics and orientations. The effect of getting a job through WIN is in addition to the total R^2.

Table 4A–2
Predicting Average Economic Independence for 133 UI Fathers Who Received UI and 28 Fathers who Did Not Receive UI

Dependent Variable and Significant Predictors	UI Fathers Who Did Receive UI			UI Fathers Who Did Not Receive UI		
	t Ratio Regression Coefficient	Regression Coefficient	Beta Weight	t Ratio Regression Coefficient	Regression Coefficient	Beta Weight
Dependent Variable (1978–1979)						
ECIA Average Economic Independence	—	—	—	—	—	—
Background Characteristics (1978)						
Other Adults Working Part-time, 1978	—	—	—	2.3	0.31	0.40
Total Number of Children, 1978	-2.1	-0.31	-0.16	-1.8	-0.85	-0.30
Previous Job Pay ($/week)	-3.0	-0.13	-0.24	1.8	0.0042	0.37
Orientations (1978)						
Liking of Previous Job[a]	3.0	0.20	0.24	—	—	—
3. Would Leave Welfare/UI if Payments Cut 10 percent	-2.8	-0.20	-0.22	—	—	—
11. Acceptability of Borrowing from Friends and Relatives when Necessary	-2.2	-0.19	-0.18	—	—	—
4. Welfare is Good Way of Life	-3.0	-0.45	-0.24	—	—	—

Controls						
R Race (proportion white)	0	0	0	0.1	0.05	0.02
C City (proportion Chicago)	−0.8	−0.09	−0.07	2.2	0.64	0.39
Constant Term			2.86			0.12
R² (adjusted) Background Characteristics[b]			0.05			0.21
R² (adjusted) Orientations[b]			0.18			0.00
R² (adjusted) Total[b]			0.23			0.21

[a]The following item (which does not appear in table 2–1) was rated on a four-point scale ranging from Not at All to Very Much: "Overall, how much did you like that [previous] job?"

[b]The R^2 values have been obtained by entering the control variables first in the stepwise multiple-regression equation, followed by the background characteristics, and then by the orientations. This provides a minimum estimate of the effect of the orientations and a maximum estimate of the effect of the background characteristics.

5 Causes of Marital Disruption

One of the puzzling questions regarding welfare is whether availability of these payments encourages marital disruption and thereby increases welfare dependency. It has been argued that as mothers have the opportunity to gain income in their own right (through welfare), they have less incentive to maintain a marriage.[1] It also has been argued that when a father no longer occupies the role of breadwinner in a welfare family, he feels a loss of self-esteem that leads to marital disruption.[2] Associated with the latter view is the implication that low-income fathers have little commitment to their families and are content to leave support of their families to others.

Findings from the present analysis help test these assumptions about the relationship between welfare and marital disruption. Our test will not be perfect because our sample includes only families already on welfare, rather than including nonwelfare families where the wife may be thinking of leaving her husband for welfare. Nevertheless, we will learn a great deal more than was known prior to this analysis. A useful introduction to the present effort is a brief review of earlier research.

Previous Evidence on Welfare and Marital Disruption

Research on the welfare-marital disruption relationship can be divided into three categories, according to the kinds of data used. The first category uses census data. Oliver Moles examines the strengths and weaknesses of several studies carried out with this kind of database. He finds the studies using different units of analysis—for example, one study using statewide relationships between family status and welfare payments with another considering the impact of welfare payments on the marital status of individuals—as well as different statistical methods. Inconsistencies in the results of these studies, therefore, is not surprising. Consistency probably could be achieved by using a common approach in subsequent research, but Moles goes on to raise serious questions about the usefulness of census data. He points out that the data generally lack important information such as psychological measures about individuals. Moreover, data on any given set of individuals are gathered at only one time. It is not possible to trace the welfare-marital status situations over time with the same persons; hence, cause and effect cannot be disentangled.[3]

The second category of research—the panel study—derives its data from repeated interviews with the same respondents. Two national studies of special importance were mentioned in chapter 1: the Panel Study of Income Dynamics carried out at the University of Michigan and the National Longitudinal Surveys carried out at Ohio State University. Moles lists the results from seven studies using one or the other of these databases. In some studies welfare causes separation or divorce, while in others welfare does not affect marital status.[4]

The basis for ambiguous results is highlighted by the recent debate between Draper and Bahr regarding their respective analyses of the National Longitudinal Surveys. The authors disagree as to whether the surveys show that welfare causes marital disruption or the other way around. Both authors agree, however, that there may be important psychological variables that influence marital disruption or acceptance of welfare that were not measured in the surveys. They also agree that there is no sure way of determining from the series of correlations derived from the data whether welfare causes marital disruption or disruption results in welfare.

This kind of difficulty arises from the fact that the surveys were not designed explicitly to study the welfare-marital disruption issue. The survey sample does not consist of current welfare recipients. Rather, it consists of several thousand females within a certain age group. Some of these women are married, others are not at the time of the first interview; some have been on welfare during the year prior to that interview, others have not. Imputations of causality based upon data from subsequent interviews become shaky as various assumptions must be made about the equivalence of these sets of women in all respects except marital and welfare status. In short, these panel studies have not completely overcome the difficulties besetting studies that collect data at only one point in time.[5]

The third category of research potentially can resolve these difficulties. It uses an experimental design. Persons are assigned at random to an experimental group that is eligible for welfare payments or a control group that is not eligible. Comparing the levels of marital disruption in these two groups should indicate whether the availability of welfare affects disruption. These conditions were approximated in the guaranteed-income experiment carried out in Seattle and Denver, which was mentioned in chapters 1 and 4. Results of the experiment are cited by Bahr and by Bishop as offering substantial evidence that a guaranteed income (a kind of welfare payment) significantly increases marital disruption.[6] Their commendation of the experiment, however, seems unwarranted.

Critique of the Seattle-Denver Experiment

We noted in chapter 4 that the Seattle-Denver families were not assigned to the experimental or control groups in a purely random fashion. Lower-income families were purposely assigned in larger numbers to the experiment, while higher-income families were assigned in larger numbers to the control group. Correction for the higher-income level of the controls was to be made by adjusting for income in the statistical analysis.[7] Ignored in this procedure is the possibility that the nonrandom assignment might introduce other differences between the two groups that were not measured and not controlled in the statistical analysis.

Suppose, for example, that lower-income families have a higher percentage of consensual marital arrangements (fewer formal marriages) than higher-income families. Suppose further that marital disruption occurs more frequently when there is a consensual arrangement. In that case, the higher rate of marital disruption in the experimental group would be the result of a greater proportion of consensual marital arrangements and not the result of the income guarantee. (Merely controlling for income in the statistical analysis would not be sufficient.)

The appropriate way to have dealt with the situation would have been to measure marital arrangements in the experimental and control groups and make any adjustments for those differences in the statistical analysis. This method would have required the Seattle-Denver researchers to have measured such arrangements. More generally, it would have required the researchers to develop a theory of marital disruption and measure key variables identified in such a theory. They failed to undertake that task, ignoring not only a measure of marital arrangement, but also such measures of social psychological variables as the feelings of the marital partners for each other and feelings of stigma toward the guarantee.[8,9]

This failure to try to understand the reasons why marital disruption occurs opens another possible flaw in the Seattle-Denver effort. The systematic difference between the experimental and control groups might be associated with different bases for marital disruption. That is, the factors that cause marital disruption among the lower-income families with the guaranteed-income option might be different from the factors influencing disruption among the higher-income families acting as controls. In such a situation one could not attribute differences in marital disruption levels between the groups solely to the experimental treatment.

The caveats offered with respect to the Seattle-Denver experiment are not merely hypothetical. Marital arrangements and various social-psychological variables, including feelings of stigma, are significant predictors of marital disruption among WIN partners, as discussed in the next section. We also show that the model predicting marital disruption for welfare persons is substantially different from the model for persons applying for unemployment compensation who, in general, have higher family incomes. Although these findings and comments do not disprove the Seattle-Denver results and interpretations, they cast considerable doubt upon them.

The present research effort falls into the category of a panel study, with measures made at two different times. Unlike the panel studies mentioned earlier, all persons in the sample start out on welfare (or applying for unemployment insurance) and all start out as members of a two-parent family.

Marital Disruption Themes

The items in the 1978 questionnaire were created to measure orientations and background characteristics that were believed to be important in affecting marital disruption. Thus, orientations toward the acceptability of welfare, other forms of income such as gambling, and work were designed. One hypothesis was that there would be greater marital disruption in families where fathers perceived a conflict between the acceptance of welfare and the self-esteem they gained through work.

The extent to which marital partners felt committed to a two-parent family also was hypothesized to affect the marital situation along with the extent to which the partners got along with each other. Hence, orientations were created that measured commitment to family and feelings of the partners toward each other.

Various background characteristics of the marital partners and the marital arrangement—for example, whether the couple was formally married, as well as age, and previous job pay of the fathers—also were hypothesized to be potential predictors of marital disruption. This information was gathered in the 1978 questionnaire.

The most important function of the 1979 reinterview was to determine the level of marital disruption in the WIN families. It is necessary to conceptualize this dependent variable in an adequate fashion.

Measuring Marital Disruption

One could view marital disruption as a sudden and complete break in a relationship. A more realistic view is that there are different levels of disruption that can befall a marital relationship. Preceding a major dis-

ruption there are likely to be smaller disruptions. Couples who do separate at one time may reunite later. The highest level of disruption is
permanent separation of the marital partners.

Following this line of thought, marital disruption will be regarded
as a variable that has a continuous range of values from no disruption at
all to long-term separation of the partners. For purposes of this study,
the measure of marital disruption is made on the following three-point
scale:

0 = No separation of the original partners during the period from
the 1978 interview through the 1979 reinterview

1 = At least one separation between the 1978 and 1979 interviews,
but both original partners together at the time of the reinterview

2 = Original partners separated at the time of the 1979 reinterview

Each WIN and UI father was given a rating on this scale depending on
his answers to certain reinterview questions.[10] It is assumed that separation at the time of the 1979 reinterview is a more serious disruption
than having been separated during the 1978–1979 period but being together at the reinterview. One might argue that some of the fathers given
a 2 rating at the 1979 reinterview might reunite with their families later
on. This argument might be true, and if the period between interviews
was longer, a better measure disruption would have resulted. However,
it is likely that at least some of the separations observed in 1979 were
permanent, making the more extreme 2 rating appropriate.

Overall, the proposed rating procedure seems desirable because it
regards marital disruption as a continuous process in which certain realistic distinctions are made. Table 5–1 presents the distribution of marital disruption scores for WIN and UI fathers (families).

Marital Disruption Among WIN Families

The procedures used for predicting marital disruption are essentially the
same as those used in chapters 3 and 4 to predict economic independence.
One additional issue is considered in this chapter, however. Disruption
between two persons can depend upon the background characteristics
and orientations of each. The primary data gathered in this study were
from WIN fathers rather than from their wives. Hence, our analysis
begins with the orientations and characteristics of the fathers. Data were

Table 5–1

Distribution of Marital Disruption Among WIN and UI Families

(percent)

Marital Disruption (MARD)[a]	WIN Families (1979) (n = 302)	UI Families (1979) (n = 167)
0	82	78
1	10	5
2	8	17

[a]0 = No separation of original partners during 1978–1979.
1 = At least one separation during 1978–1979, but original partners together at the time of the 1979 reinterview.
2 = Original partners separated at the time of the 1979 reinterview.

gathered, however, from about two-thirds of the WIN mates. We will consider the impact of their orientations and characteristics on marital disruption after the impact of the WIN fathers' variables are examined.

Background Predictors for WIN Fathers

Figure 5–1 presents the fathers' predictors of marital disruption. (The complete results, including control variables, appear in table 5A–1 in the appendix to this chapter.) As intimated earlier, a significant predictor of marital disruption is the marital arrangement of the WIN partners at the initial interview—where a score of zero indicates that the partners are formally married in 1978 and a score of 1 indicates that they are living together on a consensual basis. It is reasonable to find that partners who are not formally married experience more disruption. One expects persons who are bound together only by informal bonds to exert less effort to stay together when difficulties increase as compared to persons bound by formal bonds.

The other predictor of marital disruption is age. The older the man, the less likely is marital disruption to occur. The same relationship is observed among couples in the American population at large.[11] It makes sense that as people get older, they tend to form more stable relationships. Although these background characteristics are important predictors of marital disruption, figure 5–1 clearly indicates that orientations are the dominant predictors.

Orientation Predictors for WIN Fathers

The six orientations that predict marital disruptions can be divided into two groups. The first two orientations deal with marital strain, and the next four with income-support issues.

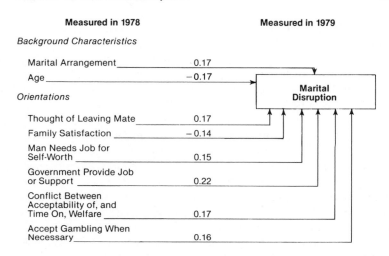

Measured in 1978   **Measured in 1979**

Background Characteristics

| Marital Arrangement | 0.17 |
| Age | −0.17 |

Orientations

Thought of Leaving Mate	0.17
Family Satisfaction	−0.14
Man Needs Job for Self-Worth	0.15
Government Provide Job or Support	0.22
Conflict Between Acceptability of, and Time On, Welfare	0.17
Accept Gambling When Necessary	0.16

Marital Disruption

Note: For a detailed presentation of the regression equation upon which this figure is based, see table 5A–1. The numbers associated with the arrows are the beta weights.

Figure 5–1. Predicting Marital Disruption for 302 WIN Families

Thought of Leaving Mate and Family Satisfaction. The two orientations that measure marital strain provide no surprises (orientations 25 and 23). It is reasonable that the more a WIN father thought of leaving his mate in 1978, the more marital disruption was experienced in 1979. His contemplated activity summarizes his feelings about his mate. Similarly, it is not surprising to find that the more satisfied a father is with his family's functioning, the less likely the occurrence of marital disruption—that is there is a negative relationship between family satisfaction and marital disruption.

Acceptability of Gambling. The more that WIN men believe gambling is an acceptable form of income (orientation 13), the higher the marital disruption experienced. Gambling is an unstable source of income, and one might expect that an interest in such an activity would undermine a family situation. The predictors of acceptability of gambling support this view. Fathers who are most accepting of gambling want others to help support their families and see external forces controlling success.[12]

Man Needs Job for Self-Worth. It was hypothesized that WIN fathers who strongly valued work and rejected welfare would feel inner conflicts at having to go on (or continue on) welfare (orientation 14). These conflicts, it was further hypothesized, would lead to marital disruption. The orientation discussed in this section and the two others following it support this hypothesis.

It was noted in chapter 4 that the belief that a man needs a job to maintain his self-worth predicted economic independence for black WIN fathers only. Here, this orientation predicts marital disruption for both black and white fathers. It is understandable that as WIN fathers believe that work contributes to their self-worth, and as they are out of work, they will feel badly about themselves. This inner conflict is likely to contribute to marital tension, which in turn fosters separation.

Examination of the predictors of this orientation support this interpretation. Thus, finding self-development through work is the strongest predictor.[13] One can appreciate how unemployment would engender conflict in a father who felt his self-development frustrated by loss of work.

A striking confirmation of how loss of jobs leads to loss of worth and frustration among low income men is seen in the WIN mothers' comments about men during the group interviews:

Social scientist:	Do you think men feel they can't think well of themselves unless they have a job?
Ann:	I think so. It all depends on the person of course. But I think in general, people in general, especially men, they have to have a job to feel good about themselves. It's the work ethic for the man.
Chris:	Men got an ego trip. If they ain't got a job, they lose their self-respect. They don't feel good about themselves.
Ann:	They are living off a woman, even though they might not mind living off a woman.
Chris:	Oh, you got some like that.
Ann:	But they like to feel like they are the men—the one who gets the job.
Betty:	I think it does something to the male, to the male himself. Society has programmed, like somebody was saying, a man is supposed to be thus and so. He's supposed to be the breadwinner, the king. He's supposed to be the ruler.
	And you know, if a man does not have his own money, go to that 9-to-5 job or whatever, it just drains him. It just does something to him on the inside.
Ann:	It does something to me on the inside, so I know what it would do to a man.

The validity of these women's insight is underlined by the following comment of a father in another group interview.

Social scientist:	Do you think your wife should help support the family if you are not working?
Bob:	Not really, no. I think she should help out as much as she can, but I do not think she should entirely support them because I wouldn't want no woman to support me.

Even though the women got their liberation and rights, I still say I'm the man. I should have more support in the house than the women do.

I feel bad if a woman makes more. If my wife makes more, it kind of irritates me a little bit. I can live with that more than, say, she just takes care of me altogether and I'm sitting around doing nothing.

Bob's comment, set in the context of the women's remarks and our statistical findings, exemplifies the extent to which American men in general, including men on welfare, identify their self-worth with being able to support a family.

Government Provide Job or Support. This orientation combines commitment to work with acceptability of adequate government support (orientation 18). The fact that high ratings on this orientation lead to marital disruption needs to be viewed in light of the WIN fathers' situations. They have no jobs and are receiving only marginal incomes from the government. Those who give high ratings are experiencing a discrepancy between what they believe the government should do and what the government is doing with respect to providing them adequate jobs or incomes. The discrepancy probably intensifies the frustration of these fathers and so fosters marital disruption.

It is of particular interest that the strongest predictor of this orientation, as for the previous orientation, is finding self-development through work.[14] Thus, there is another indication of how commitment to work and inability to find work promotes marital disruption.

Conflict Between Acceptability of Welfare and Time on Welfare. This orientation was constructed on the hypothesis that low acceptability of welfare and a considerable amount of time on welfare creates internal conflict in welfare fathers which leads to marital disruption. More specifically, the ratings from one orientation (accept welfare when necessary, orientation 8) and a background characteristic (months on welfare during the 1973–1978 period) were combined to form a new variable, conflict between acceptability of welfare and time on welfare (variable 8T). WIN fathers were given a score of 1, 2, 3, or 4on this new variable as follows:

1 = *High* acceptability of welfare *and high* months on welfare

2 = *High* acceptability of welfare *and low* months on welfare

3 = *Low* acceptability of welfare *and low* months on welfare

4 = *Low* acceptability of welfare *and high* months on welfare[15]

Fathers with high ratings on this new variable reject the idea of welfare even as they have been forced to accept welfare during the past five years. The point to keep in mind is that these same fathers are once again faced with going on or continuing on welfare. The psychological conflict they faced in the past is again to be faced in the present, which leads to marital disruption. Meanwhile, the fathers with low scores on the new variable are experiencing little psychological conflict. The fact that they have been on welfare and are going on welfare again does not violate their sense of propriety, and hence does not lead to marital disruption.

It must be emphasized that this new variable measuring conflict between acceptability of and time on welfare does not predict economic independence. Men are not staying on welfare because they accept the idea of receiving welfare. However, when economically forced to accept welfare over a period of time, those fathers who are more accepting of the idea of welfare experience less psychological conflict and less marital disruption than those who reject the idea of welfare.

Missing Orientations. It is of considerable interest that certain orientations do not appear in the model. Wanting others to support one's family, for example, is not a direct predictor of marital disruption. That orientation has a small indirect impact, because it predicts acceptability of gambling, which does have a direct impact upon marital disruption. But overall, disruption is not caused by fathers rejecting the idea of maintaining a family.

Impact of the Mates

The fathers' mates cannot be ignored as actors in the marital situation. Information was gathered from mates (as distinct from WIN mothers who were heads of their own households and results from whom were presented in chapter 3) by providing each WIN father with a questionnaire for his mate to complete and return.

Our concern here is with the mates of the 302 reinterviewed WIN fathers. A total of 204 of those 302 mates returned usable questionnaires. Responses of the 204 mates were combined with the responses of the corresponding WIN fathers to determine the impact on marital disruption of the orientations and the background characteristics of both partners.

Details of the statistical analysis are presented in table 5A–2 in the appendix to this chapter. The essential result is that only one of the mates' variables enters significantly into the prediction of marital disruption. This orientation is self-confidence (see table 2–1). The greater the self-confidence of the mate, the less likely is marital disruption. It makes sense that the mate's positive feeling about her ability to accomplish goals helps keep the family together. All the WIN father variables mentioned earlier remain predictive of marital disruption except for satisfaction with family functioning. (The mate's feeling of self-confidence is related to and displaces the variable measuring WIN fathers' family satisfaction in the predictive model.)

The fact that the major predictors of marital disruption are the fathers' does not necessarily mean that the fathers initiated the disruptions. The mates may have forced the issue. However, the orientations of the father are more crucial to the stability of the marital situation than the orientations of his mate. This is understandable in light of the fact that the major predictive orientations of the fathers relate to their inability to support their families through work. One would *not* expect the mates to feel as debilitated as the fathers about failing to support their families and having to go on welfare. And, indeed, the constructed variable that measures acceptability of and time on welfare for the mates is unrelated to marital disruption. (The data are available from the author.)

The group interviews demonstrate how inability to support his family deeply frustrates a father. A further excerpt from the group interview with the WIN mothers illustrates how this frustration can lead a number of fathers to activities that intensify marital strife:

Harriet:	And the guy starts drinking [because he's out of work]. He never drank that much before. He is constantly drinking. They are at the bar, and they find money to buy liquor.
	That's what their fights are about [with their mates]. The guy finds money to drink, but they can't get money to give to the house.
Social scientist:	That's because he doesn't have enough money?
Harriet:	But they got the money for the booze. They don't have money for the home.
Chris:	They find that five dollars to go buy that stuff to get high with. But they can't find no five dollars to buy some bread and milk to put in the house.

Betty: Because people will share the bottle and all that stuff, but they won't share a loaf of bread.

Chris: You know they can't find that money to go buy that bread and milk. But they can find that money to get the stuff they want so as to get their heads all messed up.

                    I mean that's kind of one of my problems. I say, "What's wrong with you? You can walk around here and get high. I'm the one that has to sit and worry about getting the bread and milk in the house."

Social scientist: You think some men give up after a while, get discouraged?

Chris: They go to arguing a lot. The least little thing that the wife will say to him, they jumping down her throat. He's feeling bad. He's out of work. And the wife's not working. And they wondering where is the money going to come in.

Betty: A lot of men will leave home because of that. They feel that a woman can make it on their own without him.

The women understand the feelings of failure and frustration that low-income men experience when they cannot support their families. They also feel considerable hostility toward the men when the latter try to resolve their difficulties through drink. Under the pressure of poverty and unemployment, some fathers retreat from the task of supporting their families, leaving the mother with the entire burden.

Our findings parallel those of Elliot Liebow in his classic participant-observation study of black streetcorner men. Liebow sees the men on Tally's corner living in a world of drink and promiscuous sex because of their failure to fulfill the dominant family and social values of our society.[16] George Gilder and other conservatives see this failure as the cause of difficulties in the ghetto rather than the result of other factors such as unavailability of jobs at which men can support their families. Conservatives fail to understand the importance that many poor men attach to supporting their families and the process by which they may throw in the towel on that issue because of lack of opportunity for training or jobs.

The following excerpt from a group interview illustrates the strong family commitment of some welfare fathers and the intense emotional stress that accompanies failure to fulfill the economic aspect of that commitment. Adam, who speaks first, is in his mid-forties. He has been unemployed for some time and has been told by WIN that he is too old to receive training. Chet is in his late twenties. He is a Vietnam veteran who has had training but is unable to obtain a job that pays enough to support his family.

Social scientist:	Do you think a man should leave his family if he can't support them?
Adam:	I have been with my wife twenty-three years. Right today I would not leave her. If you have a wife, to my opinion, if you have a wife, she is going to stick with you. I don't care how low you drop or high you go up. If you care about her and she cares about you, you are going to be together. You can't go too low for her. Both of you go down together.

I'm sure that if you and your wife are together, there is some way you are going to make it. There is no ifs, ands, or buts about it. There is some way you can make it.

Do I feel like I'm going to get down so low that I am going to leave my family? What am I going to leave my family when they are down for? No. Never.

Chet:	I understand what you say. You were right when you said how high you go or how low you fall, if your woman is your woman or your wife is your wife, she would take that bitter with the sweet.

So all that comes into play. If I'm dead broke, or I have a stroke, or I'm disabled, you understand, and I'm laid up, the income stops. But my wife is still thinking. I cannot deny her of her own opinion and her own thoughts, what she might want to be within herself.

She might go out and hustle. She might sell drugs. She might sell pussy. She might make flicks, you know.

I am on my back and then she comes and says, ''Here baby, take that.'' Or she comes every day, you know, and the kids are all right. First thing is the kids, you know. Because she's going to make sure that they eat and they be clothed and they try to go to school to the best of her ability.

About if a man should leave when he's that down? Well, his soul leaves. Maybe not his body, because that's within him. If he's disabled, don't you think he left? When a man is out of work, don't you think he left?

It's like I can't get out of the bind. It's like he's standing up, turning around. I can't get out of this circle. [Demonstrating.] But I know there is a way out, you know. Don't you think he left?

Excuse me, let me borrow your paper for a minute [picks up newspaper]: "Man left his wife because he was down."

[Pointing to stenotypist] This is what this guy is doing because he's a stenographer. [Pointing to social scientist] You know he wants to find out. He can complete the notes because he's the doctor, you know. But he can only complete the notes to what we're saying.

You have got to really experience it. And the system is kind of messed, which it is messed. It is like runny shit.

Chet's emotional outburst becomes partially incoherent, revealing his deep frustration at being unable to find a way out of poverty and welfare. If fathers such as Chet and Adam turn to drink or desert their families it is not because they regard their family responsibilities lightly but because they regard them very seriously.

The Paradox of Welfare

Provision of welfare to families headed by fathers has two contrary effects: it promotes stability among some families while it promotes disruption among others, depending on the psychology of the fathers. An unfortunate paradox appears. Those fathers who most strongly aspire to work their way to economic independence are the ones who tend to leave their families when that aspiration cannot be fulfilled. Men who stay with their families are those who feel most comfortable in accepting welfare. Before drawing policy implications from these findings, it is useful to compare the causes of marital disruption among WIN fathers with the causes among UI fathers.

Marital Disruption Among UI Families

There is a greater amount of disruption among the UI than the WIN fathers, as noted in table 5–1. (The UI fathers include those who received as well as those who did not receive UI benefits.) This finding might seem odd at first glance. One might expect greater disruption among two-parent families that are suffering greater economic hardship. The WIN families are certainly much lower on the socioeconomic scale than the UI families. The WIN families, however, are not having their first experience with unemployment. Poor families that could not withstand the trauma of unemployment would have broken up prior to the start of the present study. The UI families are not nearly as familiar with the trauma of unemployment and being on an income-support program (see past work activity in table 4–1). This previous continuity in work experience probably accounts for the higher disruption rate among the UI families in our sample.

Background Predictors for UI Fathers

Figure 5–2 presents the predictors of marital disruption for UI fathers. Two background predictors are related to previous work activity. The longer the UI father has been out of work, the more likely he is to experience marital disruption. The higher his previous job pay, the less likely he is to experience marital disruption.

These findings are reasonable. Among families not used to unemployment, the longer the head of household finds himself in the degrading position of being out of work (regardless of whether or not he receives UI benefits), the greater the tension in the family and the higher the probability of disruption. For men who are frequently out of work, either the family separates after a few bouts with unemployment or it adapts to the situation, as in the case of the two-parent WIN families.

It is reasonable that UI parents tend to stay together when the father

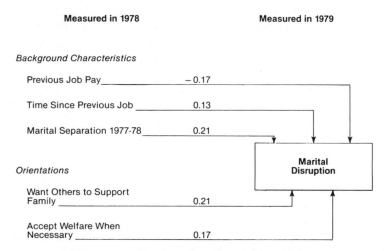

Note: For a detailed presentation of the regression equation upon which this figure is based, see table 5A–2. The numbers associated with the arrows are the beta weights.

Figure 5–2. Predicting Marital Disruption for 168 UI Families

has had high income in his previous job. The expectation of returning to a relatively high standard of living probably helps the couples overcome their current distress. When previous job pay has been low, there is no such expectation to ease the shock of unemployment, resulting in greater marital disruption.

The third background predictor of marital disruption is whether or not there was a separation of the couples during the year prior to the 1978 interview. Those who separated earlier had more disruptions in the 1978–1979 period. It makes sense that those who separated in the past and then came back together are more likely to separate in the future.

The major predictor of past separation is thought of leaving one's mate.[17] This orientation cannot be said to predict past separation in the strict sense because it was measured in 1978, whereas the separation refers to occurrences during the 1977–1978 period. It is reasonable to suppose, however, that there is a continuing feedback relationship between thinking about leaving one's mate and actual separation, so that thinking about leaving can be viewed as an indirect predictor of marital disruption for UI fathers. Thinking of leaving one's mate was a direct predictor of marital disruption for WIN fathers. This marks one similarity between WIN and UI fathers.

Orientation Predictors for UI Fathers

Two orientations directly predict marital disruption for UI fathers that are quite different from those for WIN fathers. The more that UI fathers want others to help support their families (orientation 22) and the more they accept welfare (orientation 8), the higher their marital disruption. The interpretation is straightforward. Those fathers who reject the idea of supporting others take the opportunity of unemployment to relieve themselves permanently of that responsibility by separating from their families. The meaning of these findings is more clearly seen by directly comparing the WIN and UI findings on marital disruption.

Comparing WIN and UI Results

The variables that predict marital disruption for WIN families seem quite different from those for UI families. There is some overlap as seen in table 5A–4 in the appendix to this chapter. The two predictive background characteristics for WIN fathers, age and marital arrangement, are significant for UI fathers. Also, the orientation "thought of leaving one's mate'' is significant for UI fathers (when 1977–1978 separation is not included in the analysis).

But the other five orientations that predict disruption among WIN families—including family satisfaction and the belief that a man needs a job for self-worth—are not significant in predicting disruption among UI families. (The variable constructed for WIN fathers, relating acceptability of welfare to time on welfare, is not directly relevant to UI fathers. A variable that would be relevant—relating acceptability of UI to length of time on UI from 1973–1978—proved to be insignificant in predicting marital disruption. The data are not presented to conserve space.) These findings suggest basic psychological differences between the two groups of fathers.

These differences are confirmed by noting in table 5A–4 that the two orientations predictive of marital disruption among UI families are not predictive for WIN families. The WIN fathers do not experience marital disruption because of preference for welfare or having others support their families. Moreover, WIN fathers' previous job pay and length of time unemployed do not affect their marital situation. Only 1977–1978 separation predicts marital disruption in the WIN sample (when thought of leaving one's mate is not included in the analysis).

The sharp psychological differences affecting marital disruption between WIN and UI families probably reflect the different situations in which the fathers of these families find themselves. WIN fathers at the time of the first interview had stayed with and tried to support their families under conditions of periodic unemployment and the need to accept welfare. Missing from the sample are those families which had split the first time unemployment struck and the need for welfare occurred. Hence, the fact that marital disruption among WIN families is not predicted by preference for welfare and having others support one's family may reflect the loss from the sample of families that had split before the study commenced.

The UI fathers had been more or less regularly employed up until the time just prior to the initial interview. The impact of unemployment was relatively novel for them and their families. Findings from the UI sample, as against the WIN sample, probably are more indicative of what happens to families in the general population, including low-income families, when unemployment strikes as something new and unexpected. We can say with assurance that marital disruption among two-parent welfare families is not the result of fathers' lack of commitment to supporting a traditional family. Disruption is a result of welfare fathers' loss of self-worth at being unemployed and experiencing the humiliation of accepting welfare.

UI fathers probably do not feel the same humiliation as welfare fathers at being unemployed or being on unemployment insurance. The UI program does not carry the same stigma as welfare. Even more important, the UI fathers would be aware that they could obtain a job without great difficulty. Those UI fathers who did not receive benefits, indeed, found jobs very quickly. The task UI fathers set for themselves is finding the best job available, as noted in chapter 4, not locating just any job at which they can support their families at a subsistence level. The self-worth of UI fathers is not as deeply shattered by loss of work (over long periods of time) as that of WIN fathers. Hence, variables measuring self-worth through work or time on UI versus acceptability of UI do not predict marital disruption for them. (The situation of fathers on UI at the current time, with unemployment about 10 percent, is undoubtedly more desperate than in 1978–1979.)

Summary and Conclusions

Unemployment has a significant impact on marital disruption. For UI fathers the impact is direct. Length of time out of work and low earning capacity leads to marital disruption. For WIN fathers, the impact is indirect, mediated by orientations toward work and welfare. That is, marital disruption is caused by WIN fathers' negative feelings about being out of work and accepting government support as a substitute for a paycheck.

The negative impact of unemployment and low earnings on marital stability, along with the positive impact of length of time married, was found to be significant in the University of Michigan panel study.[18] (In our analysis, age of the WIN father is closely related to, and replaces, the time-married variable in predicting marital disruption.) The University of Michigan study, however, failed to measure orientations related to the marital situation. As a result, the study explained very little of the marital separation observed. Results from our study show that orientations contribute a major amount of explanation of marital disruption.

When public policy is aimed explicitly at increasing unemployment (for example, to control inflation) the costs should be evaluated not merely in terms of increased dollars for unemployment insurance and welfare benefits, but also in terms of the social and psychological costs of family disruption. Conversely, increased employment for fathers of poor families should increase marital stability. More generally, it seems likely that significant numbers of families on welfare that are now headed by women would have remained, or would have become, economically independent two-parent units if the fathers had been able to obtain adequate employment.

Our research findings also illuminate the effects of another potential public policy—providing a nationwide guaranteed income. The Seattle-Denver researchers' claim that a guaranteed income promotes family disruption is placed in a different context by our findings. First, the empirical findings of the experiment might result from researchers having ignored the possibility that disruptions were greater among families whose partners were not formally married and more of these families might have been in the experimental group.

Second, to the extent that a guaranteed income causes marital disruption, our findings suggest that the reasons involve the stigma fathers experience in accepting that income, rather than their mates' preference for heading their own households as suggested by the Seattle-Denver researchers. The implication that has been drawn from the dubious interpretation of the Seattle-Denver researchers is that a guaranteed-income policy should be abandoned because it causes disruption among otherwise sound families.[19] The implication to be drawn from our findings is that a guaranteed-income policy is inferior to an employment policy.

This study also shows that marital disruption is also affected by the feelings that the marital partners have toward each other. Public policy is not likely to affect those kinds of feelings. There will continue to be families headed by a single parent because people do not get along with one another. A number of those families will be candidates for welfare. Chapter 6 considers the comments of welfare recipients on the positive and negative aspects of government-support efforts.

Notes

1. See, for example, Michael T. Hannon et al., "Income and Marital Events: Evidence from an Income-Maintenance Experiment," *American Journal of Sociology* 82 (1977), 1186–1211.

2. See, for example, George Gilder, Visible Man: *A True Story of Postracist America* (New York: Basic Books, 1978), pp. 243ff.

3. O. C. Moles, "Public Welfare Payments and Marital Dissolution," *Divorce and Separation,* ed. G. Levinger and O. C. Moles (New York: Basic Books, 1979), pp. 167–180.

4. Ibid.

5. See the following discussions based upon analyses of the Ohio State University national longitudinal data: Stephen J. Bahr, "The Effects of Welfare on Marital Stability and Remarriage," *Journal of Marriage and the Family* 41 (1979), 553–560; Thomas W. Draper, "On the Relationship Between Welfare and Marital Stability: A Research Note," *Journal of Marriage and the Family* 43 (1981), 293–299; Stephen J.

Bahr, ''Welfare and Marital Dissolution: A Reply,'' *Journal of Marriage and the Family* 43 (1981), 300–301; and Thomas W. Draper, ''Reply to Bahr,'' *Journal of Marriage and the Family* 43 (1981), 302.

   6. Bahr, ''Welfare and Marital Dissolution: A Reply''; and J. Bishop, ''The Negative Income Tax Experiments: Some Reflections on Their Implications for a Theory of the Family,'' *Economics and the Family,* ed. S. J. Bahr (Lexington, Mass.: Lexington Books, 1980), pp. 95–121.

   7. Michael C. Keeley et al., ''Design of the Seattle-Denver Income-Maintenance Experiments and an Overview of Results,'' *A Guaranteed Annual Income,* ed. Philip K. Robins et al. (New York: Academic Press, 1980), p. 20.

   8. Hannon et al., ''Income and Marital Events.''

   9. Hannon et al., ''Income and Marital Events,'' p. 1195. Also see Leonard Goodwin, ''Limitations of the Seattle-Denver Income-Maintenance Analysis,'' *American Journal of Sociology* 85 (1979), 653–657; and Michael T. Hannon et al., ''Reply to Goodwin,'' *American Journal of Sociology* 85 (1979), 657–661.

   10. The WIN and UI fathers were asked in 1979 whether they were presently living with the same mate as in 1978; if they were, they were asked whether they had separated at all since the last interview because of family problems; they were also asked to identify their current marital status.

   11. Leonard I. Pearlin and Morton A. Lieberman, ''Social Sources of Emotional Distress,'' *Research in Community and Mental Health* (Greenwich, Conn.: JAI Press, 1979), vol. 1, pp. 217–248.

   12. Predictors of accept gambling when necessary (orientation 13) preceded by their beta weights are as follows for WIN fathers:

Background Characteristic
−0.12 Age

Orientations
   0.24 Want others to support your family (orientation 22)
   0.20 Accept social security or pension (orientation 12)
   0.16 Success through external forces (orientation 27)
   0.12 Have family problems
   0.09 Accept welfare when necessary (orientation 8)

R^2 (adjusted) total $= 0.17$

   13. Predictors of man needs job for self-worth (orientation 14) preceded by their beta weights are as follows for WIN fathers:

Background Characteristic
−0.10 Other adults working part time

Orientations
    0.30 Self-development through work (orientation 28)
    0.22 Government provide job or support (orientation 18)

R^2 (adjusted total) = 0.14

14. Predictors of government provide job or support (orientation 18) preceded by their beta weights are as follows for WIN fathers:

Background Characteristic
    0.10 Months on welfare 1973–1978

Orientations
    0.41 Self-development through work (orientation 28)
−0.13 All right for mother to work (orientation 16)
    0.10 Accept government support when necessary (orientation 10)

R^2 (adjusted) total = 0.24

15. *High* and low ratings were determined respectively by a father being above or below the mean value given for the variable by all reinterviewed WIN fathers. A high rating for accept welfare when necessary is a value greater than 2.32; a low rating is a value equal to or less than 2.32. A high months-on-welfare rating is greater than 13; a low rating is 13 months or less.

16. Elliot Liebow, *Tally's Corner* (Boston, Mass.: Little, Brown, 1967).

17. Predictors of marital separation 1977–78 preceded by their beta weights are as follows for UI fathers:

Orientations
    0.33 Thought of leaving mate (orientation 25)
−0.16 Family satisfaction (orientation 23)

R^2 (adjusted) total = 0.16

18. Isabel Sawhill et al., *Income Transfers and Family Structure* (Washington, D.C.: Urban Institute, 1975), p. 39.

19. Kenneth J. Neubeck and Jack L. Roach, "Income Maintenance Experiments, Politics, and the Perpetuation of Poverty," *Social Problems* 28 (1981) 308–320.

Appendix 5A
Complete Models of
Marital Disruption for
WIN and UI Fathers

The complete model (regression equation) for marital disruption among WIN families, using WIN father predictors, appears in table 5A–1. Given the distribution of the dependent variable—many zero scores indicating no marital disruption—a tobit analysis was conducted along with an ordinary least-squares (OLS) analysis. The same rationale presented in the appendix to chapter 3 applies here.

The complete model for marital disruption among UI families, using UI father predictors, appears in table 5A–2.

The marital disruption model for WIN families that uses both the fathers' and the mates' predictive variables appear in table 5A–3. The mates' self-confidence orientation replaces the WIN fathers' family satisfaction predictor; otherwise the model is the same as that for the fathers alone except for small changes in the beta weights (see table 5A–1). The results of applying the WIN father model to UI families and the UI model to WIN families appear in table 5A–4.

Table 5A–1
Predicting Marital Disruption for 302 WIN Families by Tobit and Ordinary Least-Squares Analyses[a]

Dependent Variable and Significant Predictors	Tobit Means on Variables for Respondents		t-Ratio for Regression Coefficient[b]		OLS	
	MARD score = 0 (n = 248)	MARD score = 1 or 2 (n = 54)	Tobit	OLS	Regression Coefficient	Beta Weight[c]
Dependent Variable (1978–79)						
MARD Marital Disruption	0.0	1.44	—	—	—	—
Background Characteristics (1978)						
Age in 1978	33.3	27.7	−3.8	−3.3	−0.011	−0.17
Marital Arrangement (proportion living with mate but not married)	0.09	0.18	2.5	3.2	0.32	0.17
Orientations (1978)						
25. Thought of Leaving Mate	1.75	2.14	2.6	3.3	0.12	0.17
23. Family Satisfaction	2.86	2.68	−2.3	−2.6	−0.14	−0.14
8T. Conflict between Acceptability of Welfare and Time on Welfare	2.54	2.80	3.1	3.3	0.11	0.17
14. Man Needs Job for Self-worth	2.66	2.98	2.6	2.9	0.10	0.15
18. Government Provide Job or Support	3.12	3.34	3.4	4.2	0.31	0.22
13. Accept Gambling when Necessary	1.36	1.62	2.8	3.0	0.15	0.16
Controls						
Race (proportion white)	0.38	0.39	0.8	0.2	0.01	0.01
City (proportion Chicago)	0.48	0.61	0.6	1.1	0.07	0.06
				−1.12		

Constant Term

Probability of MARD = 0 (no marital disruption) for WIN fathers giving same scores to predictor variables that were given by WIN fathers who did not have marital disruption (see first column of figures for mean scores). ... 0.90

Probability of MARD = 0 (no marital disruption) for WIN fathers giving same scores to predictor variables that were given by WIN fathers who had marital disruption (see second column of figures for mean scores). ... 0.64

R^2 (adjusted) Background Characteristics[d] ... 0.05
R^2 (adjusted) Orientations[d] ... 0.15
R^2 (adjusted) Total[d] ... 0.20

[a]Tobit and OLS analyses were carried out on the INSTAT computer program developed by Dr. Joseph Tu when he was at Brookings Institution.

[b]Predictor variables are considered to be significant if they exhibit t ratios in both the OLS and tobit analyses that are 1.64 or greater (see columns 3 and 4), indicating a probability of 0.10 or less of these variables having no predictive effect.

[c]The beta weights are useful in indicating the relative importance of the predictor variables in explaining the dependent variable. Each weight is determined by multiplying the regression coefficient by the ratio of the standard deviation of the predictor variable divided by the standard deviation of the dependent variable.

[d]The R^2 values have been obtained by entering Race and City first in the stepwise multiple-regression equation, followed by the background characteristics and the orientations. This provides a minimum estimate of the effect of the orientations and a maximum estimate of the effect of the background characteristics. Total R^2 is the effect of background characteristics and orientations.

Table 5A–2
Predicting Marital Disruption for 167 UI Families by Tobit and Ordinary Least-Squares Analyses

Dependent Variable and Significant Predictors	Tobit Means on Variables for Respondents		t Ratio for Regression Coefficient		OLS	
	MARD score = 0 (n = 130)	MARD score = 1 or 2 (n = 37)	Tobit	OLS	Regression Coefficient	Beta Weight
Dependent Variable (1978–1979)						
MARD Marital Disruption	0.0	1.78	—	—	—	—
Previous Job Pay	223	174	-2.6	-2.3	-0.00154	-0.17
Time since Previous Job (weeks)	1.8	2.8	1.7	1.8	0.039	0.13
Marital Separation 1977–1978 (proportion separated)	0.09	0.30	2.5	3.0	0.52	0.21
Orientations (1978)						
22. Want Others to Support Your Family	1.20	1.45	2.1	2.9	0.42	0.21
8. Accept Welfare when Necessary	1.71	2.05	2.2	2.4	0.16	0.17
Controls (1978)						
R Race (proportion white)	0.46	0.27	-0.8	-1.0	-0.12	-0.08
C City (proportion Chicago)	0.55	0.43	-0.3	-0.5	-0.06	-0.04
RUI Received UI 1978 (proportion yes)	0.83	0.83	0.4	0.1	0.03	0.01
RUIT Time on UI 1978–79 (weeks all respondents)	14.4	16.8	0.8	1.0	0.0061	0.08
Constant Term					-0.20	
Probability of MARD = 0 (no marital disruption) for UI fathers giving same scores to predictor variables that were given by UI fathers who did not have marital disruption (see column 1 for mean scores).			0.85			
Probability of MARD = 0 (no marital disruption) for UI fathers giving same scores to predictor variables that were given by UI fathers who had marital disruption (see column 2 for mean scores).			0.60			
R^2 (adjusted) Background Characteristics				0.11		
R^2 (adjusted) Orientations				0.06		
R^2 (adjusted) total				0.17		

Note: For discussion of statistical material in this table, see table 5A–1, notes.

Table 5A–3

Predicting Marital Disruption for 204 WIN Families by Tobit and Ordinary Least-Squares Analyses Including the One Significant Mate Predictor

Dependent Variable and Significant Predictors	Tobit Means of Variables for Respondents		t-Ratio for Regression Coefficient		OLS	
	MARD score = 0 (n = 167)	MARD score = 1 or 2 (n = 37)	Tobit	OLS	Regression Coefficient	Beta Weight
Dependent Variable (1978–1979)						
MARD Marital Disruption	0.00	1.41	—	—	—	—
Background Characteristics (1978)						
Age	33.4	28.1	−3.2	−3.0	−0.012	−0.19
Marital Arrangement (proportion living with mate but not married)	0.10	0.24	2.9	4.0	0.44	0.25
Orientations (1978)						
26. Self-Confidence, Mate's Rating	3.10	2.93	−2.2	−2.8	−0.23	−0.17
25. Thought of Leaving Mate	1.97	2.49	1.9	2.3	0.09	0.14
8T. Conflict Between Acceptability of Welfare and Time on Welfare	2.58	2.81	1.9	3.6	0.13	0.22
14. Man Needs Job for Self-Worth	2.71	3.11	3.5	3.8	0.16	0.24
18. Government Provide Job or Support	3.14	3.34	2.0	2.4	0.21	0.15
13. Accept Gambling When Necessary	1.38	1.68	2.3	3.1	0.17	0.19
Controls (1978)						
Race (proportion white)	0.40	0.51	2.0	1.0	0.07	0.06
City (proportion Chicago)	0.47	0.68	0.6	1.1	0.08	0.07
Constant Term				−0.82	0.02	
R^2 (adjusted) Mate's Contribution						
R^2 (adjusted) Father's Contribution					0.22	
R^2 (adjusted) Total					0.24	

Note: For discussion of statistical material in this table, see table 5A–1, notes.

Table 5A–4

Applying the Model Predicting Marital Disruption (MARD) for WIN Families to UI Families and Model for UI Families to WIN Families

| | WIN Fathers | | UI Fathers | |
Independent Variables	Own MARD Model t Ratio (Beta Weight) (n = 302)	UI MARD Model t Ratio (Beta Weight) (n = 302)	Own MARD Model t Ratio (Beta Weight) (n = 167)	WIN MARD Model t Ratio (Beta Weight) (n = 167)
Background Characteristics (1978)				
Age in 1978	-3.3 (-0.17)	—	—	-1.9 (-0.16)
Marital Arrangement (living with mate but not married)	3.2 (0.17)	—	—	1.8 (0.14)
Previous Job Pay ($/week)	—	0.5 (0.03)	-2.3 (-0.17)	—
Time since Previous Job (weeks)	—	1.0 (0.06)	1.8 (0.13)	—
Marital Separation, 1977–1978	—	3.5 (0.20)	3.0 (0.21)	—
Orientations (1978)				
25. Thought of Leaving Mate	3.3 (0.17)	—	—	2.4 (0.20)
23. Family Satisfaction	-2.6 (-0.14)	—	—	0.2 (0.02)
8T. Conflict between Acceptability of Welfare and Time on Welfare	3.3 (0.17)	—	—	—
14. Man Needs Job for Self-Worth	2.9 (0.15)	—	—	0.7 (0.06)
18. Government Provide Job or Support	4.2 (0.22)	—	—	-0.3 (-0.02)
13. Accept Gambling when Necessary	3.0 (0.16)	—	—	0.3 (0.02)

22. Want Others to Support Your Family—Male	—	0.4 (0.02)	2.9 (0.21)	—
8. Accept Welfare when Necessary	—	-0.2 (-0.1)	2.4 (0.17)	—
Controls (1978)				
Race (proportion white)	0.2 (0.01)	-1.2 (-0.07)	-1.0 (-0.08)	-1.2 (-0.11)
City (proportion Chicago)	1.1 (0.06)	2.2 (0.13)	-0.5 (-0.04)	-1.1 (-0.09)
Received UI 1978 (proportion Yes)	—	—	0.1 (0.01)	-0.1 (-0.01)
Time on UI 1978–1979 (weeks; all respondents)	—	—	1.0 (0.08)	1.1 (0.10)
Constant Term	-1.12	-0.08	-0.20	0.51
R^2 (adjusted) Background Characteristics	0.05	0.03	0.11	0.06
R^2 (adjusted) Orientations	0.15	0.00	0.06	0.04
R^2 (adjusted) Total	0.20	0.03	0.17	0.10

Note: For discussion of statistical material in this table, see table 5A–1, notes.

6

Recipients Talk of Government Help

The statistical findings have shown that the WIN program helped a small percentage of participants find jobs. The experiences of those who did and did not get jobs through WIN are worth considering as an aid in developing future policies and programs that will resolve more adequately the welfare problem. Two excerpts from the group discussions exemplify WIN experiences. (The observations of the WIN fathers are excerpted from the same group interview quoted in chapters 3 and 5; the WIN mothers' observations are extracted from the group interview cited in chapter 3.)

Fathers Talk of WIN

Social scientist: Anybody want to comment on your experiences with WIN?

Nate: When I first started going to WIN, I was just really going there to uphold my public assistance grant. But then, like every time I went there, I would get the same old story, "Yes, go check this job out."

They give me jobs that they had there for like months, you know. "Go check this job out." Nine time out of ten it turned out to be more of a hassle-type thing.

I was staying on Staten Island and I had to go all the way into Brooklyn, you know. If you are late for whatever reason, that's a setback. It was like an all-day thing in itself.

It turns out, like I said, that was my initial feeling, it turns out I got a good job out of the WIN program.

Social scientist: You did?

Nate: Yes, because the supervisor there pulled me over to the side one day. Every time I came, I had the same attitude. Some of the jobs, you know, you are, well, overqualified for, but like I said, I don't have no pride, I was ready to take any job.

You would go there and they would send you places where the people really weren't briefed as to what you were coming there for. They just treat you like you came off the street, you know. You wasn't really properly introduced.

Like, you know, I'm the type of person that I really don't like that. If they are going to send me somewhere, at least tell the man, "Well, this person from the WIN program," but like they sent me a couple of places where people looked at me, "What are you doing here?"

Social scientist: What job did the supervisor get for you?

Nate: They hooked me up on a nice job out at the Staten Island Hospital. That was up my alley anyway. I was going to school for medical technology. Like once I got there, my initial job was working in medical records.

I kept talking to the lab supervisor, and they got me a job in the lab as a laboratory assistant.

Social scientist: Was it the supervisor who took some special care?

Nate: I had got to be so delinquent down there at the WIN office. Like every time I would come, they would say, "Okay, what is your excuse now?" They more or less sensed that I wasn't interested in the program at all.

So, I guess, you know, not being special or nothing, she just pulled me over to the side, because I always had to go to her anyway to get approval for my check. She knew my kind by heart. So we rapped one day and she said, "What are your intentions? What do you want to do?"

So, one day I just received a letter in the mail, and, you know, it started out as a training program and developed into a job, at a pretty nice rate too.

Adam: I believe that some people you talk to take all the manhood out of you. You can go to some of the investigators in those places, they talk to you like you are some kid. I mean, they will take the manhood from you.

They're sending you a letter telling you that you got to be there or your check will be cut off. Then, you get there and they talk to you like a dog.

I don't care what I am getting. I don't have to take that kind of talk off of nobody. I'm a man. You are going to stand there and talk to me like I'm a child because you got a job and I'm less fortunate that I don't have one. I feel to myself that I am just the same as you are, I just don't have a job.

Just because I don't have a job, I don't say I am going to let myself go down.

Oscar: I was going to the WIN program for a couple of years. I went into different training in Manhattan. I still didn't get no job. In order for me to keep my relief, I had to go to these things every day. After all these things, I still didn't get no job.

I was a window cleaner for about twenty years. I got hurt. I still can work, but I cannot, you know, I can't clean windows no more in my life. Maybe on the ground, but not high up like I used to do. I was a guard, and I have been in the service, and I had a couple of guard jobs.

They sent me on a couple of jobs. I went way out there by Coney Island, just to sweep the floor and pick up the garbage. They sent me to the job. I was supposed to get the job. When I got there, he hired some white guy just before me. I don't think that's right.

The three men participating in the discussion illustrate general kinds of experiences with WIN. Nate and Oscar express a common feeling found in the group interviews that going to WIN is "more a hassle-type thing." It's something you have to do, but not something that you expect much to come from. Adam accentuates this point with an expression of hostility at staff people talking down to him, taking "all the manhood out of you."

Nate, on the other hand, had a positive experience with WIN staff when the office supervisor took a special interest in his situation and helped place him in a job that he wanted. Nate is a person who is perhaps more talkative and aggressive in terms of getting a job than the other fathers; he tells how after getting the job, he "kept talking to the lab supervisor" until he finally got a job as a laboratory assistant. Thus, there are some who can make use of their WIN job placement to move upward in the occupational structure.

A more typical experience expressed by the WIN fathers is that of Oscar, in which he travels to a job interview, presumably arranged by WIN, only to find the job—sweeping the floor—already filled. One can recognize the strong element of discouragement that comes with that kind of experience. Given that WIN found jobs for only 18 percent of the fathers in our sample, it is understandable that many of them would have little use for the WIN program.

Mothers Talk of WIN

Social scientist: Who would like to start with their comments on WIN?

Judy: Well, they didn't do too much for me but have me run back and forth. That's all they did for me is have me come. I had to report in and go back.

Paula: I felt the same way. I had to be there whenever they sent the letter. If I wasn't there they threatened to take you off of Aid or whatever. There was times that I just couldn't make it. And if I wasn't there, that meant no check the next time.

                 I think it was senseless to go there, because they really didn't do anything. You just sit there for a couple of hours and they interview you and it's the same thing every time you come back.

Kathy: My appointment was supposed to have been for 9:00. I was there at 8:30. They didn't call me until 10. I was sick. I told them I was sick, and I am on medication. So she said you have to sit and wait your turn. Well, it's the same questions over and over and over. They didn't help me.

Nancy: I had a different experience. I had to go down there and apply with WIN. Okay, I did. They gave me a test and asked me what I could do, or did I really want to go to school. Upon completion of the test, they decided to send me to the DeVry Institute of Technology.

                 I went over there, took a test there. It took me a while. They showed me the school. I passed that test and I ended up entering DeVry Institute of Technology. I was there two years. I just graduated from there in February, and I am proud of myself. Right now, I am seeking employment as an electronic technician.

Judy: They tested me too. I know I passed it. But I never heard from them.

Nancy: Sometimes it's the counselor.

Mary: I just got a job through WIN.

Social scientist: What sort of work is it?

Mary: Security.

Judy: Is that a security thing like guards? They told me about that too.

Mary: Well, when I went in I said, "I'm here for a job, whatever you have. I have three children, no husband, he just walked out. I need work." So beggars can't be choosey.

Paula: So you feel you're better off working?

Mary:	Yes. I'm a whole person.
Paula:	Is it worth it for you?
Mary:	It is worth working, yes.
Paula:	Do they supply the babysitting for your children?
Mary:	For the first three or four months, I think she told me. I think like the other lady says, it has a lot to do with people. It's the people working behind the desk and the person, the client that walks in the door.

The program itself is definitely needed. I pray to God you never take it away. Because women that are married and devoted their lives to their marriages and their husbands have left them, they have no training whatsoever. The WIN program provides that for them.

You have women that left school at an early age, no education whatsoever. WIN is desperately needed.

I have had the type of people you are talking about, who ran you around. Nobody can run you anyplace if you don't want to be ran around. I've also had files misplaced. I make sure I know where my files went. So, when I did go back and they could not find my files, I found my files for them.

We've got to be patient on our end, and they've got to be patient on their end. I guess on the whole, I'm saying that WIN is definitely needed and has done some definite good.

A vividly remembered feature of the WIN experience for both fathers and mothers is the way they were treated by WIN staff. On one hand, when WIN applicants feel that staff have no respect for them, they react strongly and negatively to the program. On the other hand, when they believe that WIN staff are trying to help, they react positively to the program. (In some cases, not reported in the excerpts, respondents say that the psychological support they received from the WIN experience gave them the confidence to go out and get their own jobs.)

On the Demise of WIN

WIN staff cannot be expected to feel and act positively when they know that they cannot help many of the persons assigned to them—only 9 percent of WIN mothers and 18 percent of WIN fathers got jobs through WIN. Given the scarcity of jobs at which welfare recipients can support their families above the poverty level, and given the very limited training capability of WIN, it is hard to imagine how the WIN operation could ever be more than a "hassle-type thing."

A recent report of the General Accounting Office (GAO) on WIN, based on interviews with a national sample of WIN administrators and former WIN participants, concludes that WIN has not been effective in resolving the welfare issue. It points out that lack of jobs, lack of funds for training, and inability of welfare recipients to obtain high paying jobs contribute to WIN's impotence.[1] Suggestions are made for improving WIN's reporting system. In response to the GAO document, the Department of Labor notes that WIN is to be phased out of existence. It is to be "replaced" by the current workfare and related programs of the Reagan Administration.[2]

Abolition of WIN will not solve the welfare problem. That kind of negative action does not fulfill the need for jobs and training that Mary so poignantly mentions in the group interview. Needed are welfare policies and programs that do more, not less, than WIN. In considering new policy directions, it is important to keep in mind that the level of conceptual ability of many welfare recipients is not low. Our findings (and those of others) about the limited education and job skills of welfare recipients should not carry the implication that these persons are dull-witted or lacking in ability to think beyond their day-to-day existence.

The following excerpt from a group interview with WIN fathers illustrates the conceptual sophistication of which some welfare recipients are capable despite their lack of formal education. The excerpt also illustrates again how close the life goals of welfare recipients are to those of the rest of us.

WIN Fathers Talk of Government Job Guarantees

Social scientist: Do you think the government ought to guarantee jobs for people?

Fred: Right, because they reap the resources and they collect the taxes and, therefore, in paying taxes all citizens should have a position of employment in order to keep that type of circle going on.

Food, clothing, and shelter should be a natural thing. Nobody asked to be born or to be here. We happened here. So those things should be guaranteed. In an environment that prospers and that's supposed to be prosperous and right, that should be a guaranteed, natural thing.

Just like when you come into this world, it's guaranteed that you are going to breathe air, you know. Even if you have to learn how to breathe poisoned air, some type of way you're supposed to come out and breathe. So, therefore, the government should be the same type of way. Nobody should be worried about poverty.

George: I disagree with you. When a man starts looking at the government in that way, we are putting ourselves into a hole. As a matter of fact, if you really look at the welfare system today, it's not there to help us get anyplace. It's to hold us in one place.

And that's what we get for depending upon the government. It's not helping us. So when you start looking at the government, I mean, to do everything for us, hey man, you know that's the wrong thing. They are taking too much away from us in the first place.

Fred: Yeah man! That's what I was saying. Just right now it holds you there. But the government is supposed to help you escalate.

Social scientist: What about some of you others? What do you think about the government guaranteeing you a job?

Fred: That should be number one. When you are going to have a central form of government with one head, it should be that each citizen should have a role in survival in society as well as the next-door neighbor. Therefore, it would not be no atmosphere of keeping up with the Joneses.

Harry: No, but you're creating a dictator that way.

Fred: No dictator. It can change as it wants to.

Harry: You start telling the government to take care of you and give you a job. . . .

Fred: If you're going to lay down your life and your son's life and now your daughter's life, why not let them take care of you?

Harry: If the government took care of us all, like I said, it would be a dictatorship.

Fred: But you are the government.

George: Those are only benefits from services rendered. Those are benefits the government gives us. . . .

Fred: But those are services that you render. You as people, as citizens. Those are your rights that should be given to you.

Ike: There's no way the government can guarantee 2 billion jobs. I don't know what the population of the United States is, but how can they guarantee that?

Fred: According to its resources. It's like that. They can do it.

John: But if the government gave you the job, it's going to make you lazy.

Fred: But how lazy can you be when you ask this man for a job and he asks you, "Do you have a degree? Have you been in this situation before?" And if it's no, he says, "I can't use you." You're cast out upon the street with nothing.

                But when you're guaranteed, hey, you'll be trained and you'll be learned how to do it. How will that make you lazy, unless you don't want to come? Then you can become an outcast and you can split.

John: That's what would happen. They would become an outcast. If the government gives you a job, and it's a good-paying job, and he done trained you and everything, and you go to this job, and you work this job for a while, then you got to think, "Well, I'm tired of this."

                The government got the opportunity to give me another job whether I like it or not. So, I'm going to leave this alone and I'm going to go to the government again and get me another job.

                Get trained for that, and it's going to go on down the line. Pretty soon before you die and whatever you are going to get lazy and say, "I don't want to work no more." And that's it.

Fred: But before you die, you got a bunch of training and you can go into any different type of markets just like that. If the government would open the doors and guarantee you that choice. Hey, I get tired of this, let me check that out.

                You should be able to go from here to there whenever you get frustrated. That way employers and employees would keep a nice calm balance. When you are forced into one thing, you get confusion. I'm going to battle you because you are trying to keep me there and that's where I don't want to be.

John: Now, they don't say that you have to stay at this particular job that you get. If the government has a job, of course, they should try to offer up the job for the many people that's out of work now, today.

Fred: Today as well as tomorrow.

John: We are talking about the present, now.

Fred: We are talking really for tomorrow.

John: Well, it's still the present.

Fred: We are still trying to solve tomorrow's problems too!

John: When you get tired of one job. . . .

Fred: You should be able to move into another one.

John: But what about the other one, what about the other person?

Fred: There's millions of people. It's a steady change. He comes up and picks up what I don't want to deal with. When he gets tired. . . .

Kevin: That's why a lot of people are out of work now, because they get tired of their jobs and sometimes they just quit without another job.

Fred: Well, the money should pay enough to where you should be able to get away at a certain time. I am not talking about just traveling domestic. You should be able to deal with international travel as well, see the economy of the other worlds.

Kevin: I don't know what kind of a job you're talking about or what kind of an income you're talking about.

John: We're not talking about international travel.

Les: I do think he's asking too much myself; because, you know, I haven't worked in a long time and here I am. I've got a government job.

Fred: You're speaking from a gratitude point. You're not speaking from a stand-off point as a citizen type or role. You're just saying, "Hey! I finally found love and I'm going to hold onto it."

Les: Well, it's not like that because I've been out of work for so many years. And, I finally decided to go get me a job and that's what was offered. I didn't graduate from school at all. I didn't like school that much.

Fred: Einstein didn't like it either.

Les: I know I can make things better for myself. And now I can do it. I know this job can be a source of boosting me off.

Fred: That's the way you feel.

Les: That's the way it'll be.

Fred:	Do you know that there's a market for you tomorrow to get another job?
Les:	Let me tell you what I did. If I lose this job, it won't be because the government got rid of me. It'll be because of myself.
Social scientist:	Do you think that job will lead you anywhere?
Les:	You see, I'll be certified after six months. I've got a month left to go or a month-and-a-half left to go. If I make it through that, I do think I can do what I plan to do.
Social scientist:	Are you going to get promoted?
Les:	I don't care if I get the promotions or not. I'll do something outside of the job to make myself prospective good money if that's the case.
Social scientist:	Another question I'd like to ask is whether a man really can't think well of himself unless he has a job.
Fred:	In today's society, no. You got to work. You got to work to think well of yourself.
George:	Frankly, it's very hard because I have found, in the black community, a woman can get a job quicker than a man can. I really feel that it's either the city or government's fault. I mean a woman can get a job easier. Now, as far as being in the market for a man's work, it's hard. That's probably why we are here.
Mike:	Well, let's not just consider the black community. My wife got a job faster than I did.
George:	You're not really looking at the whole thing. I mean, it's hard to see everything.
Mike:	Most jobs right now are computerized jobs. Women get them faster because men ain't trained for them.
Kevin:	Well, in a lot of cases, you have the husband and wife—there may be jealousy between them. Sometimes the woman who's the head of the household rather than the man.
Mike:	Well, that's what I have. My wife makes more than me.
John:	But what you fail to realize, though, is that in the man's vows it said, "for better or for worse." Whether you think she is supporting you or not, that still does not make you less of a man. The type of man that wants a job, he is going to get out there and look for it.

So will that woman. That woman will do the same thing. She'll get out there and she will look. Now, those men that think they are less than a man, those are the ones that are not looking for a job. They don't want a job. They just want to sit up and try to collect any kind of income they can.

The woman is going to look for her a job to take care of those in her household, even though the man in the household ain't working. That's just like me. I'm not working today. But that still don't make my wife or my children think less of me as a man. They are going to have respect either way it goes, if I got a job or not.

Kevin: It's society that looks down on you because you don't have a job.

Fred: That's why I am saying, the government should provide; everybody should be able to get a job.

Discussion of why the government should or should not guarantee jobs reveals considerable complexity of thought. The critique of Fred's ideas by the other WIN men—that such a proposal implies a dictatorial government or that it will make persons lazy—raises concerns that other, more-educated Americans would have as well. The ability of these welfare men to grasp and apply sophisticated ideas is revealed in the excerpt, even as their lack of formal education is revealed in their language. One suspects that under different circumstances many of these fathers could have achieved much higher status in the job market than they have.

Also revealed in the conversation is the practical orientation of most of these men. They are not seeking "pie in the sky." Rather, they are focusing their efforts on obtaining and keeping a job that allows them to support their families.

Toward the end of the excerpt John mentions that one should not think less of himself because he is unemployed as long as he is looking for a job. However, based on our statistical findings about expectations and experience as well as other comments from the group interviews indicating the discouragement that comes with failure in the job market, it is likely that repeated rebuffs in the job market eventually undermine men's efforts in looking for work and trying to maintain a family.

The statistical findings of this study and the group interviews reveal a sense that the present welfare system and job-training efforts without jobs are not allowing many recipients to fulfill the goals of economic independence and marital stability. New policies and programmatic efforts are needed to lower the welfare rolls. The next chapter proposes efforts that derive from the findings of the present study and stand in contrast to current conservative policies.

Notes

1. Comptroller General of the United States, *An Overview of the WIN Program: Its Objectives, Accomplishments, and Problems* (Washington, D.C.: General Accounting Office, June 21, 1982), pp. 12–13, 21–23.

2. Ibid., pp. 60–61.

7

Resolving the Welfare Problem

The most difficult step in resolving certain social problems is to see the problem clearly. The welfare problem over the years has been viewed from a distorted perspective. Policymakers and researchers have tended to focus on issues of welfare costs, benefit levels, and work requirements while having little understanding of the social psychology of the people involved. Poor persons in general and AFDC recipients in particular have been something of a "black box," an unknown, into which policymakers and economic researchers could project, as they pleased, various psychological assumptions—for example, that recipients prefer welfare to work or that psychological orientations have no influence on action—to justify or discount certain policies.

This book has sought to redress the scarcity of knowledge about the social psychology of poor people on welfare. Results reported here must be taken with particular seriousness because they are based not only on what persons say about work, government support, and family, but also on the relationship of these expressions to persons' subsequent work activity and marital status. Relevance of the research findings for matters of policy can be brought into focus by returning to the queries raised in chapter 1 and briefly summarizing the answers that have been found.

Summary and Significance of Research Findings

1. Does preference for welfare or rejection of work keep welfare recipients out of the work force?
    No. Acceptance (or rejection) of the idea of welfare or work has no effect upon the achievement of economic independence by welfare recipients judged able to work. There is virtually no evidence that welfare dependency is caused by preference for welfare.
2. Why do some welfare recipients work their way to economic independence while others continue on welfare?
    Low ability to command sufficient wages in the job market and length of time on welfare contribute to failure to achieve economic independence. Psychological orientations related to work effort also have a strong impact. High or low expectations to achieve economic independence lead to high or low levels of achieved independence.

These expectations are strongly and directly affected by experiences of success or failure in the work world. In addition, welfare fathers who express high need for supportive services show low achievement of economic independence; welfare mothers who show middle-class aspirations for retirement income from social security and job pensions achieve high economic independence.

3. Does the Work Incentive (WIN) program help participants achieve economic independence?
    Yes. When WIN finds jobs for participants they achieve a greater level of economic independence than would be expected from their background characteristics and orientations. But WIN finds jobs for relatively few participants.

4. Does the welfare experience increase persons' dependency on welfare?
    Yes. Length of time on welfare contributes to WIN persons' failure to achieve economic independence. But this time on welfare is related to low ability to obtain adequately paid jobs, not to preference for welfare.

5. How does welfare affect the marital stability of two-parent families?
    Welfare has a mixed effect. For fathers who reject the idea of welfare, the receipt of welfare benefits causes frustration, which leads to marital disruption. For fathers who accept the idea of welfare, receipt of this benefit maintains family stability.

6. Does the social psychology of UI applicants differ from that of welfare recipients with respect to achieving economic independence and marital stability?
    Persons who receive unemployment insurance, unlike those who receive welfare, tend to stay on that program because they accept the idea of government support. Marital disruption among two-parent families applying for unemployment insurance is influenced by the fathers' unwillingness to support their families as well as by fathers' length of time out of work.

These findings, based upon a substantial research effort, can now be compared with the assumptions and welfare policies of the Reagan Administration and conservatives in general.

Conservative Assumptions Versus Empirical Reality

The conservative position on welfare is well illustrated by George Gilder. As noted in chapter 1, he presents Sam, a young black from Albany,

New York, as a case study and general example of men in the ghetto. Gilder notes:

> There are innumerable jobs that Sam could do with a little time and training. There are many jobs that he could get and do immediately. They are the sort of jobs termed menial. . . . They are the sort of jobs that cannot begin to compete with welfare.[1]

The implication is that welfare benefits remove the already small desire that poor men have to work and support their families.

A more general case along these same lines is made by Robert Carleson, speaking for the Reagan administration.

> No mix of [welfare] benefits and incentives will provide the basic human needs at an affordable cost and not discourage gainful employment.[2]

Carleson almost seems to advocate less than a subsistence level of welfare payment as a matter of policy. He backs off from such an extreme position a few sentences later: "Benefit levels should be adequate to meet basic needs at all times, but should not compete with an area's prevailing wages for those who are able-bodied."[3] Carleson assumes that the prevailing wage is high enough to support the earner and his or her family at a subsistence level. The two interrelated assumptions supporting the conservative position can be summarized as follows:

1. When welfare payments provide subsistence living, a great many poor persons will choose welfare rather than jobs—that is, many poor people prefer to have the government support them and their families rather than have to work.
2. There are ample jobs in the regular work force that allow poor persons to support themselves and their families at least at a subsistence level.

It is of considerable interest that conservatives have not provided meaningful empirical data to support these assumptions. They apparently take them as articles of faith. George Gilder, for example, talks in general terms about jobs that Sam might do, but fails to describe Sam's experiences in the work force. Whether or why he ever accepted, rejected, or quit jobs remains unexplored.

Our empirical findings suggest that men like Sam may pursue their "indolent" way of life because of low expectations of achieving economic independence through work. The low expectation may have come from previous experiences of failure in the job market or perhaps through observation of the futility of efforts of ghetto fathers (such as some of those interviewed in our study) to lift their families out of poverty through hard work. (The unemployment rate was 15 percent for black males over 20 years of age in Chicago at the start of the present study in 1978.)

We can only speculate about the meaning of Sam's experiences and actions, but by interpreting results from the present study in conjunction with results from other studies it is possible to test the conservatives' assumptions. Evidence from this study clearly points to the falsity of assumption 1. Work-eligible heads of households in the cities of Chicago and New York do not stay on welfare because they prefer that mode of existence. Further meaning can be derived from that result, which bears on the validity of assumption 2, by asking why welfare recipients show no sign of malingering whereas UI recipients tend to stay on that benefit program because of preference for nonwork income. One might argue that recipients of unemployment insurance are ''naturally'' more inclined to accept nonwork income in lieu of work than welfare recipients. Such an argument is not supported by other data from our study—for example, the mean values given to orientations measuring preference for nonwork income are not consistently higher for UI as compared with welfare recipients. A more likely explanation lies in the differences in the UI and welfare situations.

UI recipients, unlike welfare recipients, can keep their benefits regardless of additional sources of income, which often include substantial earnings from other family members. The backgrounds of UI recipients, moreover, are much more likely to attract job offers that lead to economic independence than the backgrounds of welfare recipients (see chapters 3 and 4). Hence, most UI recipients in this study, especially the fathers, could survive on the nonwork support payments at the same time that they could expect to obtain reasonable jobs when they wished. The basic economic security of the recipients was not being threatened by choosing either to remain dependent on the nonwork income or to achieve independence by going back to work.

In situations where people's vital interests are not being threatened, it is reasonable that the level of preference for nonwork income influences action. In the opposite situation, where vital interests are being threatened, it is reasonable that mere preference does not influence action. The insignificant impact of preferences on welfare recipients' achievement of economic independence, we suggest, results from recipients facing severe threats to the integrity of their families.

More specifically, preferences have no statistically significant effect on welfare recipients' actions because some recipients with strong preference for nonwork income go to work when they can earn more than the low level of welfare payments for which they are eligible. At the same time, other recipients who reject the idea of nonwork income stay on welfare because they cannot find jobs at which they can earn as much as those low level welfare payments. This interpretation suggests that assumption 2—that there are ample jobs at which household heads on welfare can support their families—is invalid. Before accepting the view that there is a scarcity of adequate jobs, three additional queries must be examined:

1.   Do welfare recipients really compare their welfare benefits with wages they can obtain in the job market?
2.   Were the benefits received by AFDC recipients in our sample at the subsistence level or were they much higher so that reasonable job opportunities were being rejected?
3.   What evidence is there that the provision of additional jobs will attract welfare recipients into the work force?

Welfare Benefits Versus Job Income

At several points in the group interviews with both welfare mothers and welfare fathers, comments were made about the relation of welfare benefits to income that could be obtained from jobs. As Adam noted in chapter 4, "They put you on a job making $3 an hour, you're not on a job. People on welfare is getting that much." Adam's remark provides a positive answer to the first query, illustrating the comparisons made between job and welfare payments. That remark also seems to exemplify the problem that Robert Carleson mentioned earlier: provision of adequate benefits discourages work effort. The "advantage" of lower welfare benefits becomes apparent. If Adam received the equivalent of only $1 per hour in welfare benefits, he would be glad to accept a job paying $3 per hour, or even $2 per hour. In terms of lowering welfare costs and filling low-paid jobs, a policy of lowering welfare benefits might seem desirable.

     This kind of policy is in effect in the state of Mississippi, where a welfare family of four in 1980 was allowed only $120 per month in cash benefits.[4] Survival on that amount of money, even with food stamps and even in Mississippi, is difficult to imagine. A black member of the Mississippi legislature noted some years ago: "During the cotton-picking season no one is accepted on welfare because plantations need cheap labor to do the cotton-picking behind the cotton-picking machine."[5] Drastic lowering of welfare benefits can lower welfare rolls and costs, but the social consequences force heads of households into jobs that do not allow them to support their families at a subsistence level. Such a possibility seems totally undesirable.

The opposite situation in which welfare benefits are very high must also be considered. If the welfare benefits received by our AFDC samples in Chicago and New York were much above subsistence, the interpretation of the statistical results we have just offered would lose much of its force. Heads of households would be on welfare because of economic profit rather than necessity. That is, they would be out of the work force because they could not qualify for jobs that paid as much as the very high benefits received from welfare. It is of interest, therefore, to determine whether welfare benefits paid in Chicago or New York in 1979 were markedly above subsistence level.

In discussing welfare benefits, it is important to understand that each state sets its own "level of need" at which a welfare family of a given size is supposed to be able to survive. The level of need may be based on a national poverty index, but it is rare to discover any effort to determine whether the welfare benefits do in fact provide a subsistence income.[6] In the end, the level is determined by political factors in the state. Inasmuch as poor people wield little political power, it is very unlikely that welfare benefits would be set above subsistence level.

In 1979 the maximum cash welfare payment for a family of four in Chicago was $333 per month. The corresponding figure for New York City was $476.[7] The official poverty index for 1979 for a family of four was $618 per month.[8] Welfare recipients were also eligible for food stamps. The cash value of those stamps would bring recipients closer to the poverty index. Miscellaneous benefits such as housing subsidies would further improve the incomes of some families. (While medical service is available to all recipients, it provides no income for daily necessities.) The poverty index in any case was derived in a manner that understated the income required for subsistence. Needed are studies of the actual costs of subsistence living in relation to welfare benefits. A rare study of this kind in selected locales of New Jersey found that welfare recipients received only about 71 percent of a subsistence income.[9] New Jersey welfare benefits fall in between those of New York and Chicago. Assuming it was as expensive to live in those two cities as in New Jersey, it appears that welfare recipients in those cities were not living above a subsistence level.

In response to the second query then, the economic benefits which members of our AFDC samples derived from welfare were not high enough to discourage them from taking jobs that allowed them to support their families at least at the subsistence level. These findings underline the point that subsistence-level welfare payments do not promote malingering or serve as a work disincentive. They also support our interpretation that lack of adequate jobs is a major cause of welfare dependency.

To test further the adequacy of that interpretation, and answer the third query, the results of offering special jobs and training to welfare recipients will be examined.

When Jobs Are Offered

Five thousand jobs were created for AFDC recipients as part of a federally funded Welfare Demonstration Project (WDP) during the 1972–1974 period.[10] The jobs were in public agencies and private nonprofit organizations located at twelve sites in four states. The jobs were mainly in personal service and clerical areas. They were meaningful jobs, as distinct from make-work activities, often involving union affiliation. Workers received paychecks from the agencies, not from the welfare office as in the case of work-for-relief (workfare) programs. There was an overflow of candidates fo the WDP jobs, with twice as many AFDC persons screened as selected. How many more welfare recipients would have been interested in the jobs had recruitment been more intensive is not known.

As part of the evaluation of WDP, a sample of work supervisors of the welfare participants were surveyed. Eighty percent of the 150 supervisors surveyed rated WDP participants at least as efficient and willing to learn as regular employees. Ninety percent of the welfare participants surveyed reported an increased feeling of confidence about obtaining and holding permanent jobs.

The WDP effort was not meant to provide permanent employment but rather to help welfare recipients make a transition to unsubsidized employment. At the time of the final evaluation survey in 1974, 80 percent of the WDP participants had been terminated from the program, but only about half that group had found unsubsidized employment. The percentage of people who found unsubsidized jobs may have dropped even lower as the final 20 percent of the sample still in WDP were forced to leave. That is, extensive stay in WDP probably was the result of welfare recipients being unable to locate equivalent jobs in the regular labor force.

The level of wages of those WDP participants who did find jobs was about the same as the wage level of the comparison group of welfare recipients who had not participated in WDP. Thus, termination of the public-employment experiment left welfare participants about where they started: many of them unable to find jobs at which they could support their families, and those who were employed getting the same wages as others with similar backgrounds. The fact that these welfare recipients did flow into the subsidized jobs when they were available and did carry them out effectively, however, substantiates our view that labor-market limitations are a major cause of the welfare problem.

Another large-scale public-employment demonstration project was carried out in New York City. Participants were recipients of home relief, persons who received local relief funds because they had no dependent children and so were not eligible for AFDC. This Work Relief Employment Project (WREP) began in 1973.[11] During the first year of operation, over 14,000 job assignments were made in city agencies from a pool of 25,000 persons who were ready to go to work. As with WDP, the limit to the program was set by the number of jobs available rather than the persons who wanted jobs.

Interviews with job supervisors showed the WREP workers were judged to be as productive as regular workers. Supervisors indicated, moreover, the WREP workers were above average in willingness to learn and ability to get along with co-workers. WREP workers themselves reported high satisfaction with their jobs. They especially liked receiving paychecks from the city agency rather than checks from the welfare office.

The WREP demonstration, as with WDP, was not meant to provide permanent employment; it was to help welfare recipients enter the regular, unsubsidized work force. The transition from subsidized to unsubsidized employment was not very successful. As with WDP, relatively few WREP workers (only about 25 percent) were able to move into the regular work force. Here again is evidence that welfare recipients can and will work successfully in adequate jobs, but that many cannot find similar jobs in the regular work force. Inasmuch as the welfare recipients performed well in their subsidized jobs, the low level of transition to unsubsidized employment seems to result from a lack of job opportunities rather than an unwillingness to work or a need for training. The results of these two public employment experiments provide the answer to the third query. One might believe, however, that a modest increase in training would lead welfare recipients to markedly higher levels of employment without the need for additional new jobs.

When Work-Training Is Offered

A major experiment involving about 1,600 randomly assigned AFDC mothers was initiated in 1976 at several sites across the country.[12] The objective of this effort was to provide these mothers with a supported work situation involving supervised subsidized employment for as much as twelve to eighteen months mainly in clerical areas and paying somewhat more than the minimum wage. The job experience and training were supposed to enhance these mothers' ability to find unsubsidized jobs and achieve economic independence. A comparison group of AFDC mothers not in the experiment also were involved in the study.

During the first three months of the experiment there was, as would be expected, a huge difference between the supported-work group and the comparison group with respect to the percentage of persons employed: 95.2 percent versus 19.4 percent. During the last three months of the experiment, when all the AFDC mothers had left supported work, the difference between the two groups was much smaller: 42 percent of mothers who had been in the experiment were employed versus 34.9 percent of the comparison group mothers. The difference of 7.1 percent between the two groups was statistically significant at the 10 percent level (one chance in ten that the difference was due to chance), but the magnitude of the difference is small.[13]

More striking than the difference in employment between the experimental and comparison groups is the steep decline in the percentage of supported-work mothers employed at the beginning and end of the experiment: 95.2 percent versus 42 percent. A familiar pattern appears: welfare persons are able to perform well in subsidized jobs but many of them cannot make the transition to the regular work force. Lack of transition occurs despite the training and job experience received.

The training, mostly in clerical skills, did not enable mothers to enter higher skilled jobs. Indeed, those mothers who were helped the most were those who had the least skills and job experiences to start with. Mothers who had some modest skills at the beginning of the experiment were not helped significantly by the supported-work experience.[14]

Training welfare mothers for low-skilled, low-paid jobs, even under the best conditions, cannot resolve the welfare problem unless there is a concomitant effort to raise the wages and increase the number of these jobs. Another possibility is to train welfare mothers for higher-level jobs. Preliminary results from a small experiment to train WIN mothers as electronic technicians reveals that some of the most able mothers can complete a rigorous eight-month training program and obtain high-paying jobs.[15] For less able mothers—that is, those with lower levels of reading and mathematics achievement—longer training periods probably would be necessary. The WIN program in general has never attempted to support training for high-quality jobs.

Assumptions Revisited

Results from the demonstration projects and the research reported in this book contradict the two assumptions noted in the beginning of this chapter that undergird conservative welfare policies. That is, we have found the following:

1. Poor people prefer to be off welfare and working, not on welfare and out of the job market.
2. There are an insufficient number of jobs at which welfare heads of households can support their families at least at a subsistence level, not ample jobs for all those wishing to support their families.

Collapse of the conservatives' assumptions means that the current policies erected on them are bound to fail. These policies center on slashing welfare benefits and having welfare recipients work for whatever benefits they receive—the imposition of workfare. It is clear enough from our findings that cutting benefits can only harm welfare familes who, already on the edge of subsistence, are doing everything they can to achieve economic independence. The harm resulting from workfare may not be so clear.

The Workfare Hoax

Three reasons are usually given in support of workfare policy.[16]

1. Workfare will discourage malingerers from applying for, or staying on, welfare.
2. Workfare experiences will improve job skills and work habits of participants and hence allow them to achieve economic independence.
3. Useful work is provided to the community in return for the money contributed to welfare recipients.

Research findings reported in previous chapters reveal no detectable number of malingerers on AFDC. Work-eligible mothers and fathers are on welfare out of necessity, not preference. The falsity of the malingering thesis is further underlined by evidence from the California workfare 1973–1974 effort. One would expect welfare rolls to decrease in the California counties where workfare was introduced if in fact there were malingerers on those rolls. That did not happen. There was no decline in the welfare rolls in those counties where workfare was introduced as compared with those counties where it was absent.[17] Robert Carleson's claim for the deterrent effect of workfare, based on 23 recipients leaving welfare in Bordentown, New Jersey, is not supported by a broader, more systematic collection of data.

The second reason in support of workfare policy is also suspect.

Experience in low-skilled supported work under benign conditions does not lead to major improvement in the employability of welfare recipients, as our previous discussion shows. An examination of workfare experiments indicates that conditions of work activity are far less benign than those in the supported-work experiment. Typically, the activities are make-work.

Workfare In Action

A fifteen-month workfare program was initiated in Massachusetts in 1978. Unlike other efforts of this kind, a careful attempt was made by researchers to evaluate its effectiveness.[18] More than 1,000 AFDC fathers were found eligible for workfare and were randomly assigned to the workfare experiment or to a control group. Those on workfare were to report to part-time activities where they would spend enough hours to justify receipt of their welfare check (not a paycheck). Those in the control group were subject to the usual welfare procedures. Nine months after the experiment began, data were gathered on the work and welfare experiences of the two groups of fathers.

Examination of the quality of the workfare assignments showed that 65 percent of the assignments required no skill at all. A welfare father who was assigned as a maintenance worker at a courthouse made a comment that the researchers termed typical: "It's not giving me any training that I can use in the future to get a good paying job."

With respect to the impact of workfare on subsequent employment, 63 percent of the fathers in the experimental group had experienced some period of unsubsidized employment during the nine months after their workfare assignment. However, 57 percent of the control group of fathers also had experienced unsubsidized employment. Statistical analysis showed no significant difference in the experiences of the two groups. Hence, there was no evidence that workfare provided significant job skills to participants or that it enabled them to achieve a higher level of economic independence than they would have achieved without the program.

The inability of workfare to provide job skills or to lower local (non-AFDC) welfare rolls was pointed out as long ago as 1961 in a nationwide study of workfare—then called work relief—by the U.S. Bureau of Family Services.[19] The bureau collected data by mail and its staff visited twenty-four welfare agencies in eleven states to observe work relief firsthand. Three findings are significant:

1. Most work-relief participants were men who had been assigned to unskilled laboring jobs.

2. Work relief did not significantly reduce the welfare rolls; it could do so only if the economy produced additional regular jobs.
3. Work-relief projects useful to the community were likely to interfere with regular employment (that is, take jobs from those in the regular workforce) and so were difficult to justify.

These findings are as applicable to the AFDC situation as the non-AFDC (general assistance or home relief) situation. Workfare generally cannot provide meaningful and useful work to recipients unless it takes jobs away from workers in the regular labor force. If that happened, workfare would have succeeded only in adding new persons to the unemployment and welfare rolls. If welfare recipients were doing useful work and were not displacing other workers, they should be paid prevailing wages for that kind of job in the form of a paycheck, not a welfare check. To do otherwise would be to exploit these people, to introduce a form of "slave" labor.

In practice, workfare consistently has provided only make-work activities. It thus becomes a way of spending administrative funds to harass heads of households who cannot find jobs that allow them to support their families and probably lowers these persons' expectations of achieving economic independence. Imposition of workfare also provides the American public with the illusion that something is being done about the welfare problem when, in fact, nothing positive is being accomplished.

Any discussion of workfare must recognize that it is not a recently discovered policy, going back only twenty or thirty years. Its articulation as a nation's policy goes back at least to Cardinal Richelieu. Upon becoming chief minister of France in 1625 he called for the creation of insitutions "in all the cities of our realm" where "able-bodied poor could be employed in public works."[20] Workhouses sprang up across Europe where the indigent were housed, fed, and clothed in return for such work as preparing materials for weaving.

In 1789 Alexander Hamilton organized the New York Manufacturing Society for the purpose of having persons work in exchange for public assistance. By 1820 the effort proved economically infeasible and collapsed. Indeed, throughout Europe and the United States, workhouses proved unable to lower welfare rolls and costs.

Workhouses disappeared because they proved eonomically and socially unsound. The reasons for their unsoundness were precisely those that make recent workfare efforts unsound. The puzzle is why such a completely discredited policy should once more capture the imagination of a national government.

From Discredited Policy to Realistic Solution

The reemergence of workfare can be attributed to the twenty-year failure
to devise a viable welfare policy in the United States and hence the
continuing presence of substantial numbers of the welfare poor. Our
urban areas are crowded with unemployed mothers who support their
families on welfare checks and "indolent" and "unmotivated" men who
hang around streetcorners. To the casual observer it makes sense that
these persons should do something for their welfare benefits.

Unknown to the casual observer, but recognized in this present study,
is that many welfare mothers and fathers have struggled in the job market
for years to maintain their families. However, they have been unable to
obtain or maintain those jobs that would allow them to raise their families
permanently out of poverty. Also generally unobserved are the negative
experiences of these men and women in taking entry-level jobs to find
that there was no advancement or that the jobs were temporary. The
feelings of failure and discouragement that flow from these experiences
are not without effect.

A central finding of our study is that as persons fail to achieve
economic independence through work, their expectations of achieving
such independence are lowered, which in turn lessens their pursuit of
employed work. Another important finding is that lack of employment
and the need to accept welfare causes conflict in many fathers and promotes marital disruption. Hence, the observed apathy among poor men
and the large number of welfare households headed only by mothers
emerges from the inability of these persons to locate jobs. These people
do not need the temporary, make-work activities of workfare. They need
adequate training and jobs; jobs that pay enough for them to support their
families at least at a subsistence level and that are relatively secure. The
lesson for welfare policy is clear: provide work, not welfare.

From Social Maintenance to Employment Emphasis

Although welfare policy will remain impotent without an aggressive em-
ployment policy, the federal government has shown great reluctance to
intervene directly in the job market. Only under the duress of the Great
Depression has the government moved to create massive number of jobs.[21]
Even those efforts were far short of the need. It was the U.S. entry into
World War Two that brought full employment.

Since World War Two the government has made sporadic efforts to provide jobs when unemployment was high. The Welfare Demonstration Project (WDP) mentioned earlier was created under the Emergency Employment Act of 1971. Such efforts were meant as modest temporary efforts, certainly not efforts to provide jobs to all who wished to work. Legislative mandates committing the government to full employment have been remarkable only for their lack of effect. The 1946 so-called Full Employment Act and the 1978 Humphrey-Hawkins Act talked about employment but yielded no new jobs.[22]

If employment policies and programs have been underdeveloped, programs that might be called "social maintenance" have mushroomed since the Great Depression. These programs include welfare and unemployment insurance, as well as social security, food stamps, housing subsidies, and medical care for the poor and the aged. These programs maintain the social and economic status of persons who have lost the ability, for one reason or another, to earn enough money to pay for needed social services. Development and expansion of these efforts has been the strength of the Democratic Party.

The presidential election of 1980, however, indicates public disenchantment with the burgeoning costs of these programs. Cuts in many of these maintenance programs can be made by conservative political leaders because the public is no longer convinced that the poor should receive as much emphasis (and resources) as in the past. Findings in this book support that trend inasmuch as the blind continuation of a maintenance-welfare strategy merely keeps people on the welfare rolls. But findings in this book also argue for an alternative policy emphasis that tends to be ignored by conservatives: the need for employment policies and programs.

Conservatives see no need for special employment policies and programs because an economy unfettered by governmental controls supposedly can provide ample jobs for all. Growth of the welfare rolls during the 1960s when the economy was expanding, as well as results from the present study, and from the demonstration projects, testify to the inadequacy of the employment opportunites in our society, except when we are on a war-production schedule.

The argument for explicit employment policy resides not only with helping the poor, but with helping our society as a whole meet the challenge of new technological change in a creative and productive fashion. We are currently undergoing a new kind of industrial revolution in which the computer is invading all aspects of our life and work.

Technological Impact on the Job Market. Many low-skilled jobs and even high-skilled jobs will continue to be removed from the job market by sophisticated computers, computer-guided robots, and word processors. The disappearing jobs include operation of industrial and office machines (as the typewriter is replaced by the word processor), machinists, draftsman, and even certain computer programming operations.[23] A specific case in point is the replacement of many thousands of automobile workers by computer-guided robots.[24]

The new jobs associated with advancing computer technology will be for designers of computers and computer systems and for technicians to maintain and repair electronic equipment. Even the technician jobs will require substantial training and skill. There will be fewer opportunities for unskilled workers to find jobs at which they can support a family. There is likely to be an increasing number of candidates for welfare as a result of changes in the employment structure in the United States unless job opportunities, job training, and job retraining are implemented on a national scale.[25]

By viewing the welfare problem as one of inadequate job opportunities for low-skilled workers, it properly becomes part of a larger problem that our society faces in the wake of continuing technological advancement. Specific employment problems and potentialities will vary in different locales depending on the local employers, labor force, tax base, and residential patterns.

Outline of Policies. A New York City program to affect the job market adequately and to provide the necessary training and supportive services for workers would be different from a program designed for Chicago because of the different characteristics of the two cities. Chicago, for example, has a much higher proportion of blue-collar workers than New York. Chicago has a less segregated job market than New York, where many blacks are concentrated in service jobs. Residential segregation in Chicago is much more extreme than in New York.[26] Each of these differences suggest the need for different strategies for developing needed jobs, training, and supportive services.

Adequate strategies for locales can emerge when local employers, neighborhood representatives, city officials, labor union representatives, and others come together. Out of the common deliberations and efforts of these groups in a given locale, a plan might emerge to encourage new business endeavors in low-income neighborhoods. Such an effort would be consonant with the Reagan administration's designation of certain geographical areas as "Enterprise Zones." However, the administration proposes to provide no more than tax breaks to businesses that enter those zones.[27] That kind of help is clearly insufficient. An adequate infrastructure for business is required in these areas, including adequate roads, sewers, and fire and police protection.[28] A federal policy providing that kind of support, along with technical advice on development plans, and evaluations of the efforts made could be valuable in improving employment opportunities in inner cities.

A number of other federal policies also could be considered, such as Nathan Glazer's suggestion to increase the attractiveness of low-wage jobs by federal subsidization of medical insurance[29]; subsidized day-care centers in the inner cities to provide both jobs for some mothers and the opportunities to go to work for others; selective job-creation efforts in accord with proposals developed by given locales; and tax rebates to heads of households who work full time but do not earn a subsistence living.[30] Many other proposals could be considered. There are also difficulties associated with efforts to create new jobs, including possible inflationary effects.[31]

It is beyond the scope of this study to delve into the details of a comprehensive employment policy. However, employment problems already are with us—the welfare problem is basically one of inadequate training and job opportunities—and they will increase as computer technology advances and our economy shifts even further toward producing services rather than goods. At issue is whether a coherent, effective national approach to employment is developed or the problems are met in a scattered, ineffective manner that leads to further inceases in the welfare rolls and the need for more social maintenance services.

We look forward to the time when people who find themselves unemployed can go to a local office where they will be sure of obtaining a job or training for existing jobs at which they can support their families at least at the subsistence level. Given these opportunities, we expect on the basis of the research and other findings presented here that persons will flow off the welfare rolls into the work force. At the same time there will always be some heads of households who cannot work or be trained because of such reasons as having to care for a family member or having severe physical or psychological disabilities. These household heads could apply for AFDC as at present. AFDC would remain a means-tested program providing subsistence-level benefits determined by realistic measures of the loal cost of living.

As governmental resources are shifted to providing opportunities for people to help themselves through their own work effort, the need for social maintenance payments—such as welfare, food stamps, and housing subsidies—should markedly decrease. Payments would still be needed for the few families who continued on AFDC and for persons unable to work because of old age or disability.

In recent years, liberals have supported the provision of a guaranteed income as a means of providing poor people with sufficient income in an unstigmatized fashion. Conservatives opposed such income on the grounds that it would depress the work activity of poor people and would be extremely expensive. Results of the guaranteed-income experiment in Seattle and Denver seemed to confirm the worst fears of conservatives. As pointed out in chapters 1, 4, and 5, however, the design of the experiment was so deficient that no firm conclusions can be drawn from the results. If in fact a guaranteed income did cause some labor-force withdrawal among recipients, that would not necessarily be bad. It would open up jobs for others.

There are major drawbacks in a guaranteed income as the key component of a welfare program: it tends to relegate low-skilled persons to permanent obsolescence and idleness, and it causes marital disruption in families where the father is strongly work-oriented but unable to find adequate employment. It becomes a way of ''paying off'' and forgetting the poor, rather than a way of allowing them to participate in the mainstream of society. This study has shown that poor heads of households want to support their families through work, not through government largesse. They wish to be active, productive citizens. Policymakers have this same goal. The way to achieve that goal and resolve the welfare problem is through a training and employment strategy, not through a subsistence income strategy.

Future Directions for Policy Research

We pointed out in chapter 1 a severe limitation in the extensive and expensive research studies on poor people directed by economists. The studies regarded the actions of people as determined solely by their background characteristics, such as educational level. Their psychological orientations toward situations were considered irrelevant to their actions.

Chapters 3, 4, and 5 have shown that psychological orientations cannot be ignored as causes of action. Even when such background characteristics as educational level and length of time previously employed are included as predictors of economic independence, psychological orientations have an additional major impact on level of independence achieved. We have found, indeed, that there is a feedback effect between expectations of success or failure in the job market and actual experiences of success or failure.

The nature of the feedback relationship between orientation and experience needs more extensive exploration. Although expectations may be markedly affected by immediate experiences in the job market, other orientations may be affected only after a long period of experience. For example, acceptance of middle-class forms of income support (social security and job pensions) that influence achievement of economic independence among WIN mothers might be influenced by early family experiences rather than later experiences in the job market. The point in any case is that models predicting the impact and evolution of public programs should allow exploration of the feedback relationships between orientations and actions.

Using Multiple Methods

It is important to move beyond just statistical validation of results. Statistical models can appear reasonable, yet ignore crucial factors influencing the actions of persons. For example, the models in the guaranteed-income experiment ignored social-psychological considerations. The use of the group interviews in this study exemplifies an additional technique for checking the validity of statistical results. The spontaneous discussions among small subsamples of welfare recipients tend to support and to amplify the meaning of statistical findings.

Another step could have been taken as well. Participant-observation studies might have illuminated the day-by-day experiences of a small subsample of persons participating in our welfare study. It would then have been possible to cross-check results from the statistical model with results from both group interviews and participant-observation data.

Use of these multiple methods also allows policymakers and others a clearer insight into the meaning and significance to be attributed to the results of each method. For example, statistical results indicated the debilitating effect of not being able to find adequate employment among WIN participants in general; the group discussions underlined this debilitating effect by expressions of keen disappointment when jobs terminated unexpectedly after a few months. If a participant-observation study of employment experiences had been carried out, some additional insights might have been generated as to how to improve the longevity of a WIN person's employment.

Expanding the Research Effort

Another suggestion for future research is an expansion of the research model itself. The importance of viewing the actions of recipients of public policies—the welfare recipients—in a more adequate manner has been demonstrated. We also need to consider the actions of policymakers and administrators of public policies in the research model. These persons also have psychological orientations that influence their actions, and those actions yield experiences that feed back on their orientations and subsequent policy actions. It is of considerable interest to understand how and what policymakers and administrators learn as policies are implemented and results analyzed.

A final suggestion bears on the fruitfulness of group interviews. It would be useful to conduct and analyze such interviews with persons at different levels of the policy process—that is, with policymakers and administrators of these policies—as well as recipients of the policies. It also might be useful to bring together some members of these different groups to discuss welfare policy. I have suggested in an earlier book the advantages of conducting such discussions under the auspices of a publicly sponsored research organization.[32] As social scientists expand their models and methods, they can become more effective as scientists and as persons who are helping to resolve social problems.

Conclusions

From the perspective of our research findings, it is futile to believe that the welfare problem is caused by fathers or mothers who prefer welfare to work. There are no significant number of recipients judged able to work who fall into that category. There are significant numbers on welfare because they lack the skills to obtain jobs at which they can support their families. Failure to obtain adequate jobs causes persons to lose confidence in their ability to succeed in the work world, which in turn leads to longer stays on welfare. The welfare experience itself decreases recipients' likelihood of achieving economic independence; hence, there is good reason to try to help people to leave welfare.

The socially productive way of resolving the welfare problem, according to our findings, is to allow recipients to experience success in the job market. Recipients in that way will not only gain income that will take them off the rolls, but will experience a psychological boost that will help them stay off welfare. For large numbers of low-skilled persons to experience success, jobs must be available along with adequate training programs and supportive services. Serious nationwide efforts in all these areas simultaneously will not only help current AFDC recipients but will prevent an influx of new welfare recipients as technological advances continue to eliminate low-skilled jobs.

The computer revolution is making it less likely that unskilled workers can find jobs at which they can support their families above a subsistence level. Public policies promoting high-level training—for example, in areas related to electronics and computers—along with increased job opportunities in other areas will help resolve the larger problem of adapting our society to technological change even as they resolve the welfare problem.

Help for the poor in the recent past generally has meant provision of subsidies for obtaining the necessities of life through such measures as welfare or food stamps. These subsidies ameliorate immediate distress but do not necessarily enhance people's abilities to achieve economic independence or to hold their families together. The poor need the training and the opportunity to help themselves through employment in an expanded job market. The importance of this conclusion lies in the fact that it emerges from an extensive research study, not from armchair speculation. There is good empirical reason to believe that increased employment will increase the stability of low-income families and sharply decrease the number of families headed by mothers who apply for welfare.

Providing poor people with greater employment opportunities does more than keep them off the welfare rolls. It allows a greater variety of citizens with a greater variety of talents to contribute to the development and strength of our society. Formulation of appropriate plans for increasing job opportunities and training in population centers across the country requires the thought and cooperation of many individuals and groups. Such efforts are in the national interest. The social, psychological, and economic benefits accruing to our country will far outweigh the costs of allowing poor persons to help themselves toward greater economic independence and marital stability.

Notes

1. George Gilder, *Visible Man: A True Story of Post-racist America* (New York: Basic Books, 1978), p. 247.

2. Robert B. Carleson and Kevin R. Hopkins, "Whose Responsbility is Social Responsibility: The Reagan Rationale," *Public Welfare* 39 (Fall 1981), 14.

3. Ibid., p. 15.

4. Office of Research and Statistics, *AFDC Standards for Basic Needs July 1980* (Washington, D.C.: Social Security Administration, March 1981), table 5, p. 10.

5. Statement of Mr. Clark (black member of the Mississippi legislature), Hearings before the Committee on Finance, United States Senate, 91st Cong., 2nd sess. on H.R. 16311, Family Assistance Act of 1970 (Washington, D.C.: Government Printing Office, 1970), part 3, p. 1552.

6. While exploring a reasonable basis for setting the basic level of need for welfare recipients in Massachusetts, Ellen Epstein reported that a number of states she contacted did not have a clear basis for establishing the level of need in relation to the actual cost of living. She also estimated

that AFDC benefits (including food stamps) left recipients in Boston at least 10 percent below the poverty level. See Ellen Epstein, *The AFDC Standard of Need In Massachusetts* (Boston, Mass.: Massachusetts Department of Public Welfare, Office of Research and Evaluation, December 1980). For a detailed study of the actual relationship between AFDC payments (plus food stamps) and the actual cost of living in New Jersey, see National Social Science and Law Project, *The Cost of an Adequate Living Standard in New Jersey* (Washington, D.C.: National Social Science and Law Project, 1981). This group found the AFDC families were receiving only about 71 percent of what was needed for subsistence living.

7. *AFDC Standards for Basic Needs July 1978* (Washington, D.C.: Social Security Administration, Office of Research and Statistics, March 1979), table 3, p. 8.

8. *Statistical Abstracts of the United States, 1980* (Washington, D.C.: Department of Commerce, Bureau of the Census, 1981), p. 483.

9. National Social Science and Law Project, *The Cost of an Adequate Living Standard in New Jersey.*

10. For the detailed report, see *Evaluation of the Emergency Employment Act Welfare Demonstration Project* (Santa Ana, Calif.: Decision Making Information, 1975), pp. 25, 27. For a summarized discussion of the Welfare Demonstration Project, see Leonard Goodwin, *The Work Incentive (WIN) Program and Related Experiences,* R&D Monograph 49 (Washington, D.C.: U.S. Department of Labor, Employment and Training Administration, 1977), p. 25.

11. For the detailed report, see *An Evaluation of the Work Relief Employment Project in New York City* (New York: Lieberman Research, Inc., 1975) pp. 26, 27. For a summarized discussion of the report, see Goodwin, *The Work Incentive Program.*

12. Stanley H. Masters and Rebecca Maynard, *The Impact of Supported Work on Long-Term Recipients of AFDC Benefits* (New York: Manpower Demonstration Research Corporation, 1981).

13. Ibid., p. 61.

14. Ibid., pp. 88–91.

15. Richard N. White and others, "High Quality Vocational Training for Welfare Women" (Washington, D.C.: Bureau of Social Science Research, 1981), p. 30.

16. For a more detailed discussion of workfare, see Leonard Goodwin, "Can Workfare Work?" *Public Welfare* 39 (Fall 1981), pp. 19–25.

17. *CWEP Evaluation: Interim Report for Period July 1, 1973 to June 30, 1974* (Sacramento, CA: State of California, Employment Development Department, undated).

18. Barry Friedman and others, *An Evaluation of the Massachusetts Work Experience Program* (Waltham, Mass.: Brandeis University, Heller Graduate School, 1980).

19. *Work Relief: A Current Look,* Public Assistance Report 52 (Washington, D.C.: U.S. Department of Health, Education and Welfare, Bureau of Family Services, 1962).

20. John A. Garraty, *Unemployment in History* (New York: Harper and Row, 1978), p. 45.

21. In 1933, the federal government created the Civil Works Administration (CWA) which was to provide 2 million nonrelief jobs. Offices were inundated with 9 million applicants. See John Charnow, *Work Relief Experience in the United States,* Pamphlet Series 8 (Washington, D.C.: Committee on Social Security, Social Science Research Council, 1943), p. 11. CWA was disbanded after four and a half months because of its high cost and high hourly rates and replaced by the Work Projects Administration (WPA). The WPA hired more than a million workers per year at less cost than CWA, but did not provide jobs for all who wished to work.

22. For a brief discussion of the history of full employment efforts up through the Humphrey-Hawkins Act, see Helen Ginsburg, "Full Employment as a Policy Issue," *Policy Studies Journal* 8 (1979), 359–68. Also see *A Full Employment Program for the 1970s,* ed. Alan Gartner and others (New York: Praeger, 1976).

23. The impact of microelectronics on the world economy and employment in all industrialized countries is illustrated by J. Rada, *The Impact of Microelectronics* (Geneva, Switzerland: International Labour Office, 1980).

24. *Wall Street Journal,* November 23, 1981, p. 1. Also see Richard C. Hill, "Transnational Capitalism and Urban Crisis: The Case of the Auto Industry and Detroit," presented at the annual meeting of the Society for the Study of Social Problems, August 23, 1981, Toronto, Canada.

25. Warren Brown, "Job Growth in '80s Linked to Computer: Experts Say Technical Training Essential," *Washington Post,* December 20, 1981, p. 1.

26. Appendix A in this book lists the ZIP codes for black and white respondents in Chicago and New York City. There is no overlap in residential area between blacks and whites in Chicago, while there is some overlap in New York City.

27. Stuart M. Butler, "The Enterprise Zone as an Urban Frontier," *Journal of Community Action* (September–October 1981), 12–19.

28. Edward Humberger, "The Enterprise Zone Fallacy," *Journal of Community Action* (September–October 1981), 20–28.

29. Nathan Glazer, "Reform Work, Not Welfare," *The Public Interest* (Summer 1975), 3–10.

30. In 1975, Senator Russell Long, then head of the Senate Finance Committee, attached an amendment to a 1975 tax bill that provided a tax rebate for heads of families with children who worked full time during the year and still had below poverty income. U.S. Congress, House, *Public Law 94-12,* 94th Cong., H.R. 2166, March 29, 1975, p. 5. This effort has not had a major impact on the poverty or welfare situation.

31. For a discussion of various factors that need to be taken into account in considering job creation, see Ralph Segalman and Asoke Basu, *Poverty in America* (Wesport, Conn.: Greenwood Press, 1981), pp. 315–35.

32. For the presentation of a model that takes these factors into account, see Leonard Goodwin, *Can Social Science Help Resolve National Problems?* (New York: Free Press, 1975).

Appendix A
Choice of Sites
and Samples

This appendix presents the methods used for choosing the two cities in which the study took place as well as the various samples of respondents. Also presented are certain characteristics of the cities.

Choosing Chicago and New York City

It was originally proposed that this study be carried out in three cities to determine whether the factors affecting economic independence and marital disruption varied markedly across cities. In view of the great cost of having three sites, it was subsequently decided to use only two sites. A number of different cities were considered. Two limiting considerations eliminated most cities:

1. There had to be an AFDC program for fathers in operation, because the sample was to include fathers as well as mothers entering the WIN program.

2. The program had to be large enough to collect data from 360 white fathers and 360 black fathers who would be entering the WIN program within a period of about four months during the summer and fall of 1978.

After careful investigation of the flow of men into WIN in various cities (by telephoning state and local WIN officials for this information) we found only three cities that offered the possibility of collecting the appropriate data: Chicago, New York, and Los Angeles. The State of California was not sympathetic to the research study, leaving New York City and Chicago as possible sites. Fortunately, the state and local officials in these two cities were interested in the study and fully provided the necessary cooperation to carry it out.

Respondents from Chicago and New York City are probably much like respondents in other northern urban areas. Findings from these cities are probably generalizable to these other areas. In any case, our sample is representative of cities with very large welfare and WIN caseloads.

The WIN and UI Samples

Interviewers for this study were stationed at each WIN office in Chicago and four of the five boroughs of New York City. (There were no WIN offices on Staten Island; welfare recipients reported to one of the Brooklyn offices.) WIN fathers and mothers entering the WIN offices were screened for eligibility. The screening process took place while WIN applicants were either waiting to see or had just seen the intake staff.

Criteria for eligibility for this study required respondents to be the head of household (either a mother or a father); have at least one child under 19 years of age living at home; be less than 60 years of age; and understand, although not necessarily read, English. The fathers had to be married or living with a mate. A room was set aside where respondents could complete the questionnaire. Respondents were told that the research study and the interviewers had no connection with the WIN program; they were not required to participate in the study; their benefits would not be affected by accepting or refusing to participate in the study; their responses would be held in strict confidence; anonymity would be maintained; and they would receive $5 for completing the questionnaire. WIN fathers were given a questionnaire for their mates and told that a $5 money order would be sent to their mates on receipt of the completed questionnaire.

WIN participants in the study included those who recently had been screened for welfare eligibility by the welfare offices and then referred to the WIN offices; had been on welfare but only recently became eligible for WIN because of such matters as their youngest child reaching six years of age; and were being recycled through WIN after not having been placed in a job at an earlier time. These distinctions among participants in our study are subsumed to some extent under the measure "months on welfare 1973–1978."

The objective was to have an equal number of black and white mothers and fathers distributed evenly between Chicago and New York City. It was not possible to fulfill the quotas exactly because of the small number of fathers entering WIN and the uneven racial distribution of entrants. The number of WIN persons interviewed in 1978 and reinterviewed in 1979 by race and city are shown in table A–1. Data regarding WIN persons who were eligible and ineligible for the study are provided in table A–2.

Interviewers for our study were stationed at the UI offices in the same neighborhoods as the WIN offices to meet the criterion that UI respondents live in the same ZIP code areas as the WIN respondents. The screening procedures and other eligibility criteria were identical for both UI samples and WIN samples. In addition, only those heads of households who were applying for UI benefits and had not been temporarily or seasonally laid off were considered for the study. The number

Table A–1
Number of WIN Fathers and Mothers Interviewed

	WIN Fathers			WIN Mothers			
	Original Quota	Valid 1978 Interviews	Valid 1979 Reinterviews	Original Quota	Valid 1978 Interviews	Sent for Reinterview[a]	Valid 1979 Reinterviews
Chicago	360	272	151	360	417	373	229
New York City	360	271	151	360	397	335	199
Total	720	543	302	720	814	708	428
Proportion Black	0.50	0.59	0.62	0.52	0.61	0.61	0.60
1978 Interviewees Reinterviewed			56%				60%

[a]During the initial interview, WIN mothers who were head of households were mistakenly oversampled; therefore 105 were randomly dropped from the reinterview list. The percentage interviewed is based on the number sent out for reinterview.

Table A–2
Eligibility and Ineligibility of 1978 WIN Applicants
(percent)

	Chicago *(n = 1,110)*	New York City *(n = 964)*
Eligible, Interview Completed	62.1	69.3
Eligible but Refused	14.0	14.4
Ineligible[a] (total)	23.9	16.3
Total	100.0	100.0
[a]Ineligible because:		
Did not understand English	8.8	13.9
Quota filled	15.1	2.4
Total Ineligible	23.9	16.3

of UI persons interviewed in 1978 and reinterviewed in 1979 by city and race are shown in table A–3. Data regarding the numbers of eligible and ineligible UI applicants for this study are provided in table A–4.

Group Interviews

The group sessions were held with persons who had completed the 1978 and 1979 survey questionnaires. Through the use of telephone and mail, persons were invited to participate in a group discussion about their welfare and work experiences at a downtown location in Chicago or New York City. Persons were told that they would be given $20 for their participation. Approximately sixteen persons were invited to each session, with an average of ten actually attending the session.

Three group interviews with twenty-four WIN fathers were held in New York City during July 1980. Two group interviews with twenty-five WIN fathers were held in Chicago during October 1980. During March 1981 three group interviews were held with thirty-two WIN mothers in Chicago. Each group session lasted about 90 minutes. The conversations were taken down by a stenotypist and also tape-recorded with permission of the participants. The names used in the excerpts are not the real names of respondents to preserve confidentiality.

Background characteristics and orientation scores of those who participated in the group interviews were very similar to those who did not. The only two significant differences were that more black WIN fathers participated in the New York City sessions than expected by chance (at the 0.05 level of probability) and WIN fathers were more accepting of welfare (orientation 8 on table 2–1) in Chicago than expected by chance.

It is important in any case not to impose statistical standards of sampling upon the group interview effort. The goal of the interviews was to determine whether persons discussed their own actions in a man-

Table A–3
Number of UI Fathers and Mothers Interviewed

	UI Fathers			UI Mothers		
	Original Quota	*Valid 1978 Interviews*	*Valid 1979 Reinterviews*	*Originial Quota*	*Valid 1978 Interviews*	*Valid 1979 Reinterviews*
Chicago	180	128	80	180	102	64
New York City	180	156	88	180	143	77
Totals	360	284	168	360	245	141
Proportion Black	0.50	0.62	0.58	0.50	0.67	0.74
1978 Interviewees Reinterviewed			59%			58%

Table A–4
Eligibility and Ineligibility of 1978 UI Applicants
(percent)

	Chicago (n = 962)	New York City (n = 1057)
Eligible, Interview Completed	23.9	28.3
Eligible but Refused	7.3	1.6
Ineligible (total)[a]	68.8	70.1
Total	100.0	100.0

[a]Applicants were considered ineligible for interviews for the following reasons:

Wrong ZIP Code	19.8	22.5
Did not understand English	7.6	1.4
Not heads of household or did not have mates	14.8	7.8
No dependent children	17.6	32.9
Temporarily unemployed	2.3	5.5
Not new UI applicant	6.7	0.0
Total	68.8	70.1

ner consistent with the statistical models of action, not to estimate how many persons interpreted their actions in one or another fashion. To be sure, if certain segments of the WIN father and WIN mother samples were not represented by at least one participant in the group interviews, then important information might be lost. For that reason, it might have been desirable to conduct more group interviews. Time and budget constraints precluded that possibility.

The variety of comments that do appear in the excerpts from group interviews in chapters 3 through 6 indicate that different segments of the WIN samples were involved in those interviews. The excerpts were chosen to present different views and experiences as well as to indicate the consensus exhibited on such issues as perceiving the welfare payments to be too low.

ZIP Code Distribution of Respondents

As previously mentioned, the UI respondents were chosen from the same or adjacent ZIP code areas as the WIN respondents. Tables A–5 and A–6 present data on the distribution of respondents by ZIP code in Chicago and New York City respectively.

The procedure for constructing these tables was as follows. First, those ZIP code areas were identified in which about 75 percent of the WIN respondents (by sex and race) resided in 1978. The percentage of UI respondents (also by sex and race) was then determined. Then, the percentage of WIN and UI respondents for the 1979 reinterview were determined for these same ZIP code areas.

Table A–5
Distribution of WIN and UI Respondents in Chicago Zip Code Areas
(percent)

	Black Fathers		Black Mothers		White Mothers		White Fathers	
	WIN	UI	WIN	UI	WIN	UI	WIN	UI
	n = 178 (n = 109)	n = 93 (n = 57)	n = 274 (n = 139)	n = 76 (n = 53)	n = 143 (n = 91)	n = 31 (n = 11)	n = 95 (n = 42)	n = 35 (n = 23)
	10.7 (10.2)	22.6 (21.1)	25.1[a] (21.7)	25.0 (28.4)	46.9[b] (41.8)	46.9 (63.7)	25.3[c] (16.6)	8.6 (8.6)
	51.6 (56.5)	34.5 (38.6)	45.6 (44.9)	34.1 (30.2)	23.8 (26.5)	16.3 (9.1)	19.0 (14.3)	22.9 (21.6)
	15.7 (14.9)	15.1 (14.1)	13.5 (11.5)	20.0 (22.3)			31.6 (38.2)	28.7 (25.9)
Totals	78.0 (81.6)	72.2 (73.8)	84.2 (78.1)	79.1 (80.9)	70.7 (68.3)	63.2 (72.8)	75.9 (69.1)	60.2 (56.1)

Note: The percentages not in parentheses indicate the distribution of black WIN and UI fathers in given ZIP code areas during the initial 1978 interview. The percentages in parentheses indicate the distribution of these fathers in the same ZIP code areas during the 1979 reinterview. The ZIP code areas for this group of fathers are those in which 78.0 percent of the black WIN fathers resided in 1978. The areas are listed by starting in the north of the city and working southward. Those ZIP code areas that are contiguous are grouped together.

1. 60644, 60624, 60612
2. 60609, 60653, 60615, 60637, 60621, 60636
3. 60649, 60617, 60628

[a]The three ZIP code area groupings for black mothers are the same as for the black fathers.
[b]The two ZIP code area groupings for white mothers are:
1. 60625, 60640, 60613, 60618, 60647, 60639, 60651, 60622
2. 60623, 60632, 60609, 60636, 60629, 60638
Only two of these ZIP codes overlap those of the black mothers.
[c]The three ZIP code area groupings for white fathers are:
1. 60625, 60640, 60613
2. 60639, 60647, 60622, 60651
3. 60623, 60608, 60616, 60609, 60632, 60629
These ZIP codes do not overlap those for the black fathers, although all but two overlap those for the white mothers.

Table A–6
Distribution of WIN and UI Respondents in New York City ZIP Code Areas[a]
(percent)

	Black Fathers		Black Mothers		White Mothers		White Fathers	
	WIN	*UI*	*WIN*	*UI*	*WIN*	*UI*	*WIN*	*UI*
	n = 145 (n = 78)	n = 81 (n = 40)	n = 226 (n = 116)	n = 77 (n = 52)	n = 171 (n = 82)	n = 61 (n = 25)	n = 125 (n = 73)	n = 75 (n = 48)
Manhattan[b]	7.0 (3.9)	9.9 (12.5)	12.1 (13.9)	13.1 (5.9)	5.7 (2.4)	3.0 (4.0)	3.2 (4.2)	6.6 (6.3)
Bronx[c]	15.4 (11.7)	23.5 (7.5)	15.4 (17.7)	20.6 (17.2)	7.8 (10.8)	12.5 (12.0)	8.8 (11.0)	5.3 (6.3)
Brooklyn[d]	43.8 (68.0)	35.7 (40.0)	32.9 (34.2)	35.5 (40.3)	20.1 (24.3)	15.5 (12.0)	32.8 (32.8)	25.4 (25.2)
Queens[e]	7.7 (6.5)	4.9 (10.0)	14.0 (11.4)	8.2 (5.7)	39.6 (29.0)	19.6 (8.0)	20.8 (13.9)	15.8 (14.7)
Staten Island[f]	4.9 (3.9)	0.0 (0.0)	0.4 (0.9)	0.0 (0.0)	5.3 (6.1)	0.0 (0.0)	10.4 (9.7)	0.0 (0.0)
Totals	78.8 (94.0)	74.0 (70.0)	74.8 (78.1)	77.4 (69.1)	78.5 (72.6)	50.6 (36.0)	76.0 (71.6)	53.1 (52.5)

[a]Percentages not in parentheses are for 1978 data. Percentages in parentheses are for 1979 data.

[b]For black mothers or fathers, all ZIP codes begin with 100 and are followed by 20, 27–29, 31–32, 35, 37, 39. For white mothers or fathers, all ZIP codes are included.

[c]For black mothers or fathers, all ZIP codes begin with 104 and are followed by 51–57, 59–60, 68, 72, 74. For white mothers or fathers, all ZIP codes begin with 104 and are followed by: 53, 56–57, 59–62, 65, 67, 69, 72–74.

[d]For black mothers or fathers, all ZIP codes begin with 112 and are followed by 1, 3, 5–6, 7, 10–13, 16–17, 21, 25, 33, 38. For white mothers or fathers, all ZIP codes begin with 112 and are followed by: 4–7, 10, 12, 18–21, 23, 27, 29, 30, 36–37.

[e]For black mothers or fathers, all ZIP codes begin with 114 and are followed by 1–4, 6, 12, 15, 18, 19, 23, 32–36. For white mothers or fathers, all ZIP codes begin with 114 and are followed by 12–13, 15–16, 18–21, 23, 32–35. Also included are ZIP codes that begin with 113 and are followed by 1–4, 6, 54–55, 58, 67–68, 72–73, 77.

[f]All ZIP codes used for WIN groups.

Several interesting findings emerge from comparing the Chicago and New York City results. Within ZIP code areas, Chicago is more strongly segregated by race than New York City. There is virtually no overlap in ZIP codes between the white and black respondents in Chicago, whereas some overlap exists in New York. Substantial proportions of the UI respondents in both Chicago and New York City live in the same or adjacent ZIP code areas as WIN respondents. Also, substantial proportions of the reinterviewed 1979 sample of WIN and UI respondents come from the same ZIP code areas as the 1978 samples.

Employment Characteristics of Chicago and New York City

Analyses presented in the text have pooled respondents from New York City and Chicago. This grouping seemed reasonable because there were no significant differences in major orientations between respondents from these two cities. Any differences between the cities that might affect predictions of economic independence and marital disruption were controlled in the multiple-regression equations through the dichotomous variable that distinguished between Chicago and New York.

Although New York City and Chicago are not very different for the purposes of our research, if one were to try to improve employment or job training in these cities certain major differences would have to be recognized. Table A–7 shows that New York City hires a greater percentage of white-collar workers than Chicago, while Chicago is more devoted to blue-collar and manufacturing activities.

Of particular interest is the predominance of blacks in service jobs in New York City. The distribution of blacks in Chicago is more uniform across all occupations. Although the Chicago distribution may seem desirable from the point of view of racial equality, it may result in higher black unemployment when the economy slackens.

Table A–8 shows the unemployment rate of blacks was about 40 percent higher in Chicago than New York in 1978. This might be the result of blacks in New York being better able to hold jobs in their more segregated service-job market, whereas they are less able to compete with whites in the other nonsegregated job markets because they are newer on the job. In any case, whites have systematically lower unemployment rates than blacks. In Chicago, black men have almost four times the unemployment rate of white men. Given that unemployment rate, one can appreciate the difficulty that the WIN program faced in finding jobs for black participants, not to mention the difficulties of these black participants locating work themselves.

Table A–7
Occupational Distribution by Employment by Sex and Race for Chicago and New York City in 1978
(percent)

	Total		Men	
	Chicago	*New York*	*Chicago*	*New York*
White Collar	49.7	59.7	36.9	50.7
Professional and Technical	15.3	17.9	13.6	16.8
Managers and Administrators	7.9	10.8	9.1	13.9
Sales Workers	4.7	6.1	4.3	6.9
Clerical Workers	21.9	25.0	9.9	13.1
Blue Collar	35.2	24.0	48.2	33.1
Craft and Kindred	10.5	7.9	17.2	13.3
Operatives (not transp.)	15.4	9.6	16.2	8.4
Transport Operatives	4.4	3.6	7.4	6.3
Non-farm Laborers	4.9	3.0	7.4	5.1
Service Workers	15.0	16.3	15.0	16.2
Totals	99.9	100.0	100.1	100.0

Source: U.S. Department of Labor, Bureau of Labor Statistics. *Geographic Profile of Employment and Unemployment: States, 1978,* Metropolitan Areas, 1977–78, tables 12–14, pp. 99–52.

[a]Less than 1 percent.

[b]The figure reported in table 14 of Geographic Profile 1978 as 27.2 percent is in error. The figure has to be 17.2 percent as reported above in order for the total percentage to equal 100. Moreover, in *Geographic Profile of Employment and Unemployment, 1979,* table 14, p. 56 (December 1980) the percentage of black service workers in Chicago is reported as 17.6 percent.

New York City and Chicago also have different racial residential patterns. In Chicago, blacks live in certain ZIP code areas irrespective of income, while whites are located in other ZIP code areas. There is a greater overlap of white and black areas of residence in New York City. Place of residence determines to some extent one's ability to get to a job, given the fact that most welfare recipients do not own cars but must depend on public transportation.

Table A–7   continued

Women		Whites		Nonwhites	
Chicago	New York	Chicago	New York	Chicago	New York
67.0	71.5	51.0	63.6	47.1	49.4
17.5	19.3	14.9	19.2	16.0	14.4
6.3	6.6	9.3	12.4	4.8	6.4
5.2	5.0	5.2	6.8	3.7	4.0
37.9	40.5	21.6	25.1	22.6	24.5
17.9	12.1	35.0	23.6	35.7	24.9
1.7	a	11.3	8.4	8.9	6.4
14.3	11.1	15.3	9.0	15.5	11.1
a	a	3.5	3.4	6.2	4.0
1.5	a	4.8	2.8	5.0	3.4
15.1	16.4	14.0	12.8	17.2[b]	25.7
100.0	100.0	100.0	100.0	100.0	100.0

Table A–8
Unemployment Rates in Chicago and New York City
(percent)

	Unemployment Rate	
	Chicago	New York City
Age 20 Years and Older		
Men	7.5	8.6
Women	7.9	7.2
Whites 20 Years and Older		
Men	3.8	7.7
Women	4.9	7.0
Blacks 20 Years and Older		
Men	15.0	11.2
Women	12.8	7.7

Source: U.S. Department of Labor, Bureau of Labor Statistics. *Geographic Profile of Employment and Unemployment: States, 1978 Metropolitan Areas*, 1977–78, table 8, pp. 35, 40 (September 1979).

Appendix B
Reliabilities of
Orientations

The starting point for developing the basic 1978 questionnaire for this study was developed and used by this author in earlier research.[1] A literature search was then conducted to discover the most recent theories and research findings regarding the relationship of background characteristics and orientations toward work, family, and welfare to actual work performance and marital disruption. From these materials, specific questionnaire items were constructed for use in the present study.

An initial version of the questionnaire was pretested on more than 100 respondents, including WIN and UI applicants in Boston, Massachusetts, and persons of different social-economic backgrounds in Worcester, Massachusetts.

The pretest results were reviewed to determine which questions were easily understood and answered by respondents. Statistical analyses were carried out to determine which questions clustered together to form orientations that were expected to be predictors of economic independence and marital disruption.

The final questionnaire for the initial 1978 interview was assembled on the basis of these considerations and the fact that it was to take most respondents no more than 30 to 40 minutes to complete. Slightly different versions were made for mothers and fathers because certain questions— for example, those describing family goals—had to be worded in a different manner. The 1978 questionnaire for mothers is presented in appendix C.

Reinterviews were conducted in 1979, approximately one year after the initial interview. Most reinterviews were conducted by telephone, with the remainder being sent by mail or conducted in person. The reinterview questionnaire was similar to the 1978 one, but shorter. Fewer orientations were remeasured in 1979 as emphasis was placed on gathering information on work and welfare experiences between the time of the two interviews. The questionnaire used for the telephone reinterviews is available from the author on request.

The first task following the completion of the 1978 interviews was to determine whether the items clustered together to form the orientations that were expected. Factor analysis was used as a technique to begin the process of item clustering. Responses from different subgroups—such as WIN mothers or UI mothers—were subjected to separate factor analyses. When respondents omitted an item, the mean value for the item given by the subgroup was inserted. Those items which were correlated 0.30 with a factor, and were not correlated that strongly with any other factor used, became candidates for members of a cluster. Further criteria for inclusion of an item in a cluster were that it add to the reliability of the overall measure, be common across subgroups where feasible, and have a reasonable psychological interpretation relative to the other items.

After the creation of clusters measuring the various orientations, it was necessary to examine the reliability of each cluster of items. Reliability of a cluster or an orientation is the extent to which one expects to obtain the same rating (for example, the mean value) from the same individuals using the same items making up the orientation. The Cronbach Alpha is used to estimate the reliability of each orientation. This estimate ranges from zero to 1 and is derived from the number of items in the orientation and the average intercorrelation among those items. A minimum level of reliability for a measure used in a research study such as this is regarded as 0.50. The actual reliabilities of orientations for the several subgroups are seen in table B–1. The lower the reliability of an orientation, the less likely is the orientation to be a significant predictor of a dependent variable. Or put another way, if an orientation predicts a dependent variable, it will do so even more strongly as the reliability of the orientation is increased.

In addition to having reliable orientations, one also wishes to have orientations that are relatively unique to allow clearer interpretations of results. Table B–1 contains the average correlations of each item in each orientation with one another and with items in the other orientations. The items constituting each orientation are more highly correlated with one another than with items in other orientations.

The cluster of items in table B–1 forming the orientation called "expect economic independence through work next year" does not have a sufficiently high reliability for UI fathers. This finding underlines the point made in the text: WIN fathers differ from UI fathers in substantial ways because of the periodic and lengthy stretches of unemployment experienced by WIN fathers. For WIN fathers, the component items of the expectation of independence next year have a common meaning, as revealed in the high correlations among them. For UI fathers, who take working next year for granted, the items do not have a common meaning.

Both WIN and UI mothers show high reliabilities for expectation of economic independence next year. Again, these findings correspond to those in the text where it was shown that WIN and UI mothers have similar models predicting economic independence.

While emphasis has been given to forming clusters of items to measure psychological orientations, it also has been recognized that individ-

Table B-1
Reliabilities of Selected Orientations and Means of Correlations Among Component Items

Orientations	Reliability[a]	Orientation Number											
		1	2	3	11	12	13	18	19	20	22	23	29
1. Expect Economic Independence—Mother													
WIN Mothers (n = 428)	68	42[b]	—	03	03	-07	-06	01	-03	—	—	07	07
UI Mothers (n = 141)	57	31	—	-06	04	-01	-01	-04	-10	—	—	-06	-06
2. Expect Economic Independence—Father													
WIN Fathers (n = 302)	68		41	04	03	-01	11	-01	—	-06	08	-01	06
UI Fathers (n = 168)	41		19	07	04	-09	03	02	—	01	06	-05	—
3. Would Leave Welfare or UI if Payments Cut 10 Percent													
WIN Mothers	64			47	06	-01	03	01	01	—	—	-06	02
UI Mothers	77			62	03	-05	02	-03	02	—	—	02	—
WIN Fathers	82			69	09	04	09	-01	—	05	06	03	02
UI Fathers	63			46	07	00	02	-07	—	00	02	-08	—
11. Accept Borrowing From Friends or Relatives When Necessary													
WIN Mothers	71				55	11	20	-01	-07	—	—	04	08
UI Mothers	81				68	20	42	-01	-06	—	—	-05	—
WIN Fathers	73				58	18	32	-01	—	-02	15	00	09
UI Fathers	74				59	19	29	-04	—	-01	03	-03	—
12. Accept Social Security or Pension When Necessary													
WIN Mothers	71					55	09	04	07	—	—	02	02
UI Mothers	77					63	08	08	07	—	—	12	—
WIN Fathers	71					55	18	09	—	10	01	-01	01
UI Fathers	69					53	01	07	—	13	-04	10	—

Table B–1 *Continued*

							Orientation Number						
Orientations	Reliability[a]	1	2	3	11	12	13	18	19	20	22	23	29
13. Accept Gambling When Necessary													
WIN Mothers	47						<u>31</u>	04	−07	—	—	03	06
UI Mothers	74						<u>59</u>	03	−14	—	—	−02	—
WIN Fathers	61						<u>44</u>	00	—	03	14	00	11
UI Fathers	57						<u>40</u>	00	—	00	07	−07	—
18. Government Provide Job or Support													
WIN Mothers	59							<u>22</u>	03	—	—	−01	05
UI Mothers	65							<u>27</u>	10	—	—	11	—
WIN Fathers	59							<u>22</u>	—	10	−05	10	02
UI Fathers	63							<u>25</u>	—	04	05	−02	—
19. Want Two-Parent Family—Mother													
WIN Mothers	54								<u>23</u>				
UI Mothers	71								<u>38</u>				
20. Want to Support Two-Parent Family—Father													
WIN Fathers	81									<u>42</u>	−11	02	−06
UI Fathers	78									<u>37</u>	−08	08	—
22. Want Others to Support Family—Father													
WIN Fathers	53										<u>22</u>	03	08
UI Fathers	53										<u>22</u>	−11	—
23. Family Satisfaction													
WIN Mothers	55											<u>29</u>	−04
UI Mothers	56											<u>30</u>	—
WIN Fathers	55											<u>29</u>	−01

		32	—
UI Fathers	59		
29. Want WIN Help with Personal Problems			
WIN Mothers	64	31	
WIN Fathers	69	36	

[a]The formula for estimating the reliability coefficient (the Cronbach alpha) is:

$$\text{Reliability} = \frac{(\text{number of items})(\text{average intercorrelation})}{1 + (\text{number of items} - 1)(\text{average intercorrelation})}$$

For a discussion of reliability and this formula, see Jum Nunnally, *Psychometric Theory*, 2d ed. New York: McGraw-Hill, 1978, pp. 190ff.

[b]The underlined numbers in the first column for each orientation are the average correlations among the items making up the same orientation. All other numbers are the average correlations among items making up different orientations. Decimal points have been omitted from all correlation coefficients.

ual items might be significant predictors of economic independence and marital disruption. For example, the single item "a man can't think well of himself without a job" (item 14) has a specific meaning that might well predict economic independence. Hence, it was kept among the potential predictors of economic independence and was significant in predicting independence for black WIN fathers and marital disruption among all WIN fathers.

It is not possible to determine the reliability of a single item by the methods used in this study. Further studies could undertake that task or develop several other items that would cluster with the single item and enhance its predictive power.

Note

1. Leonard Goodwin, *Do The Poor Want to Work?* (Washington, D.C.: Brookings Institution, 1972).

Appendix C
Questionnaire Used for
1978 Interviews

PART I. Different people have different ideas of what makes for a good or not very good way of life. Listed below are statements about different ways of life. Please circle the number next to each statement which best gives your own opinion on how good a way of life it would be for you.

		Not Very Good Way of Life	Fairly Good Way of Life	Good Way of Life	Very Good Way of Life
1.	Staying home full-time to look after your family	1	2	3	4
2.	Having a part-time job	1	2	3	4
3.	Having your children make many friends in your neighborhood	1	2	3	4
4.	Receiving welfare	1	2	3	4
5.	Having a husband who supports you and your children	1	2	3	4
6.	Having your children get a good education	1	2	3	4
7.	Having a close man friend, not a husband, who helps support you and your children	1	2	3	4
8.	Having a full-time job	1	2	3	4
9.	Being a single parent head of family	1	2	3	4
10.	Receiving unemployment compensation	1	2	3	4
11.	Having a good education	1	2	3	4
12.	Working full-time to support a family	1	2	3	4
13.	Having a family where the husband, wife, and children live together	1	2	3	4
14.	Being free to find a new partner when there are real problems in the old relationship	1	2	3	4
15.	Having plenty of money	1	2	3	4
16.	Having your children drop out of high school before finishing	1	2	3	4
17.	Not having a job	1	2	3	4
18.	Having enough money to support your children without the help of a husband	1	2	3	4

    *   *   *   *   *   *

19.	Think of your family's way of life as it is now. How good a way of life do you think it is? Please circle the one number to the right that best describes this way of life	1	2	3	4
20.	Think of your family's way of life **one year ago.** How good a way of life do you think you had then?	1	2	3	4
21.	What do you think your family's way of life will be like **one year from now?**	1	2	3	4

PART II. Different people have different opinions about work and family life. Listed below are a number of statements about work and family life. Please circle the number next to each statement which best gives your own opinion as to how much you agree or disagree with each statement.

		Strongly Disagree	Disagree	Agree	Strongly Agree
1.	When children are less than 6 years old, a mother should feel free to go to work at least part-time	1	2	3	4
2.	Members of a family can get along together if they only try hard enough	1	2	3	4
3.	A man should handle most of the problems with children	1	2	3	4
4.	Overall, I feel satisfied with our family the way it is now	1	2	3	4
5.	A husband and wife should share in making major decisions about spending money	1	2	3	4
6.	A man should leave his family if he cannot support them	1	2	3	4
7.	When children are more than 6 years old, a mother should feel free to go to work full-time	1	2	3	4
8.	I would rather be head of a family than have to answer to somebody else	1	2	3	4
9.	A husband and wife should share in handling problems with the children	1	2	3	4
10.	The best kind of family situation is where husband and wife are living together with their children	1	2	3	4
11.	A husband and wife should share in doing the housework	1	2	3	4
12.	A man really can't think well of himself unless he has a family	1	2	3	4
13.	A wife should make the major decisions about spending money	1	2	3	4
14.	Whether a family stays together is mainly a matter of lucky breaks	1	2	3	4
15.	I like the way our family handles money now	1	2	3	4
16.	A mother's first responsibility is to her children	1	2	3	4
17.	A husband should make the major decisions about spending money	1	2	3	4
18.	A woman should handle most of the problems with children	1	2	3	4
19.	A woman should help her partner provide money for their family to live on	1	2	3	4
20.	I like it when someone besides me makes the major decisions for our family	1	2	3	4
21.	It is all right for a father to leave his family if they can get more money on welfare when he is gone	1	2	3	4
22.	A woman should be able to support her family if necessary	1	2	3	4
23.	Overall, I am satisfied with the way my children are being raised	1	2	3	4

*   *   *   *   *   *

A major problem our family faces is:

24.	Getting enough money to live on	1	2	3	4
25.	Handling the children	1	2	3	4
26.	Getting along with one another	1	2	3	4
27.	Living in a bad neighborhood	1	2	3	4
28.	Sickness of some family members	1	2	3	4
29.	Living in bad housing	1	2	3	4

If you are either <u>married or living with a mate,</u> please answer questions in the box below. Others go to Part III.

		Strongly Disagree	Disagree	Agree	Strongly Agree
30.	I have seriously thought of leaving my mate in the last few months	1	2	3	4
31.	My mate and I often argue about money	1	2	3	4
32.	My mate and I do lots of things together in our free time	1	2	3	4
33.	My mate doesn't do enough around the house	1	2	3	4
34.	My mate appreciates the things I do for the family	1	2	3	4
35.	My mate and I often argue about how to raise the children	1	2	3	4
36.	Family life would be better if my mate worked harder at it	1	2	3	4
37.	I plan to stay with my mate	1	2	3	4
38.	My mate and I often argue about little things	1	2	3	4

PART III. Please give your own opinion as to how much you agree or disagree with each of the following statements about work and feelings about yourself by circling one number next to each statement.

		Strongly Disagree	Disagree	Agree	Strongly Agree
1.	Success in a job is mainly a matter of hard work	1	2	3	4
2.	In order to get ahead in a job, you need to have some lucky breaks	1	2	3	4
3.	The most important part of work is earning good money	1	2	3	4
4.	I am able to do most things at least as well as other people	1	2	3	4
5.	I am sure that life will work out all right	1	2	3	4
6.	I feel good when I have a job	1	2	3	4
7.	To me, it is important to have the kind of work that gives me a chance to develop my own special abilities	1	2	3	4
8.	Sometimes I get so angry I can't control myself	1	2	3	4
9.	A man really can't think well of himself unless he has a job	1	2	3	4
10.	Success in a job is mainly a matter of knowing the right people	1	2	3	4
11.	There are days when I just don't feel like getting up and doing any work	1	2	3	4
12.	Success in life is mainly a matter of lucky breaks	1	2	3	4
13.	Work should be the most important part of a person's life	1	2	3	4
14.	When I make plans, I am almost certain that I can make them work	1	2	3	4
15.	Hard work makes you a better person	1	2	3	4
16.	I feel useless at times	1	2	3	4
17.	Work is a necessary evil	1	2	3	4
18.	Getting recognition for my own work is important to me	1	2	3	4
19.	Most people like to work	1	2	3	4
20.	To be really successful in life, you have to care about making money	1	2	3	4
21.	I usually finish whatever I start	1	2	3	4
22.	Success in life comes mainly from having drive and ambition	1	2	3	4
23.	I wish I could have more respect for myself	1	2	3	4
24.	I like to work	1	2	3	4
25.	I can do almost anything I really set my mind to	1	2	3	4

PART IV. Please give your own opinion about how much you agree or disagree with each of the following statements about welfare and unemployment compensation by circling one number next to each statement.

		Strongly Disagree	Disagree	Agree	Strongly Agree
1.	If it weren't for welfare, a lot more women would have to put up with bad marriages	1	2	3	4
2.	Most people who get unemployment compensation could get another job if they really tried	1	2	3	4
3.	The government should guarantee a job to everybody who wants one	1	2	3	4
4.	The only way you can live on welfare is to have a job on the side	1	2	3	4
5.	When a person is out of work it's usually because of not looking hard enough for a new job	1	2	3	4
6	The government should make sure that each family has enough to live on	1	2	3	4
7.	My family would look down on me for being on unemployment compensation	1	2	3	4
8.	If I inherited enough money so that my family and I could live comfortably without ever working, I would go ahead and work anyway	1	2	3	4
9.	People who get unemployment compensation deserve it because they have worked before	1	2	3	4
10.	People tend to get used to welfare after a while and don't want to leave	1	2	3	4
11.	Because of welfare, a lot of women are free to leave their husbands if things are bad	1	2	3	4
12.	I would be willing to pay 10% more in taxes in order to guarantee that everybody could have a job	1	2	3	4
13.	My family would look down on me for being on welfare	1	2	3	4
14.	The only way you can live on unemployment compensation is to have a job on the side	1	2	3	4
15.	People should be able to get unemployment compensation when they decide to quit work for a while	1	2	3	4
16.	I think it's all right for some people to depend on welfare regularly	1	2	3	4
17.	Most people on welfare could get off by working if they wanted to	1	2	3	4
18.	My neighbors would look down on me for being on unemployment compensation	1	2	3	4
19.	People should be able to get unemployment compensation when the company they work for goes out of business	1	2	3	4
20.	Rather than providing welfare, the government should provide a job that pays just above the poverty level	1	2	3	4
21.	After one month of unemployment compensation, persons should be required to take any job that pays more than their unemployment benefits	1	2	3	4
22.	My neighbors would look down on me for being on welfare	1	2	3	4
23.	Many people are on welfare because they can't find jobs that pay enough to support their families	1	2	3	4
24.	If the government sent me as much money every week as I could earn at a regular job, I would stop working	1	2	3	4
25.	Many people in my neighborhood depend on welfare regularly	1	2	3	4
26.	(FOR WOMEN ONLY) It is better to be on welfare than depend on a husband to bring home the same amount of money	1	2	3	4

PART V. <u>Suppose</u> everyone in your family was <u>out of work</u>. **Please circle the number next to each statement which says how acceptable each way would be for you to get money for you and your family to live on.**

	Not Acceptable	Barely Acceptable	Acceptable	Very Acceptable

How acceptable would each of these be if everyone in your family was out of work:

		Not Acceptable	Barely Acceptable	Acceptable	Very Acceptable
1.	Receiving unemployment compensation	1	2	3	4
2.	Borrowing money from relatives	1	2	3	4
3.	Having the government send you enough money every week	1	2	3	4
4.	Playing the numbers	1	2	3	4
5.	Receiving welfare	1	2	3	4
6.	Borrowing money from a loan office	1	2	3	4
7.	Receiving interest from a bank account or other investment	1	2	3	4
8.	Shoplifting	1	2	3	4
9.	Receiving social security	1	2	3	4
10.	Borrowing money from friends	1	2	3	4
11.	Buying lottery tickets	1	2	3	4
12.	Receiving a pension from a company where you used to work	1	2	3	4
13.	Peddling stolen goods	1	2	3	4
14.	Borrowing money from a bank	1	2	3	4

PART VI. <u>Suppose</u> you were the head of your household and were <u>on welfare</u>. **Please circle the number next to each statement that best says how likely you would be to go off welfare if each of these happened.**

	Not at All Likely	Not Too Likely	Fairly Likely	Very Likely

If you were on welfare, how likely would you be to go off:

		Not at All Likely	Not Too Likely	Fairly Likely	Very Likely
1.	If you could get a job that paid 10% more after taxes than you could get on welfare	1	2	3	4
2.	If you could get a permanent job paying $200 a week	1	2	3	4
3.	If you could get free medical services in a job that paid as much after taxes as you get on welfare	1	2	3	4
4.	If you could get a job that paid 10% less after taxes than you could get on welfare	1	2	3	4
5.	If you could get a permanent job paying $100 a week	1	2	3	4
6.	If you could get a job with as good health insurance as you get on welfare	1	2	3	4
7.	If you could get a job that pays just as much after taxes as you get on welfare	1	2	3	4
8.	If you could get a permanent job paying $150 a week	1	2	3	4
9.	If your welfare payments were cut by 10%	1	2	3	4
10.	(FOR WOMEN ONLY) If a man was willing to support you and your children	1	2	3	4

30   **PART VII. <u>Suppose</u> you were receiving <u>unemployment compensation</u>. Please circle the number next**
31   **to each statement that best says how likely you would be to go off unemployment compensation if each of**
32   **these happened.**
33

	Not at All Likely	Not Too Likely	Fairly Likely	Very Likely
If you were receiving unemployment compensation, how likely would you be to go off:				
1. If you could get your old job back	1	2	3	4
2. If you could get a permanent job paying $200 a week	1	2	3	4
3. If you were offered a different kind of job that you could do, and it paid 10% more than your old job	1	2	3	4
4. If you could get a permanent job paying $100 a week	1	2	3	4
5. If you could get a new job doing what you did in your old job	1	2	3	4
6. If you could get a permanent job paying $150 a week	1	2	3	4
7. If you could get a different kind of job that paid as much as your old job	1	2	3	4
8. If you could get a job like the one you had before but it paid 10% less	1	2	3	4
9. If you were living with someone who was earning enough to support you and your family	1	2	3	4
10. If your unemployment compensation payments were cut by 10%	1	2	3	4

PART VIII. We would like to know a little more about the people who have completed this survey. Would you please answer the questions below by filling in the blanks or circling a number.

1. How old are you? _____ years old

2. What was the last grade in school you finished?

    8th grade or less 1

    9th, 10th or 11th grades 2

    Completed 12th grade 3

    Some college 4

    Completed college 5

3. Have you completed any other training to help you get a job, such as vocational school, or special training programs?

    Yes, I have completed other training 1

    No, I have not completed other training ... 2

4. Are you now:

    Single 1

    Married and living with your mate 2

    Married but separated from your mate 3

    Living with someone and not married 4

    Widowed 5

    Divorced 6

5a. (IF YOU ARE SEPARATED, WIDOWED, OR DIVORCED) How long have you been separated, widowed or divorced?

    _____ months _____ years

5b. (IF YOU ARE MARRIED OR LIVING WITH SOMEONE) How long have you been married or living together?

    _____ months _____ years

5c. (IF YOU ARE MARRIED OR LIVING WITH SOMEONE) During the **past year** have there been times when you separated because of family problems?

    Yes 1

    No 0

6. Who is head of your household? ....

    I am 1

    My mate is 2

    My mate and I are 3

    Another adult is 4

7a. Including yourself, how many people live in your household?

　　　Number in my household　　　_____

7b. How many of these people are:

　　　Children 5 years old or younger　_____

　　　Children 6 to 11 years old　_____

　　　Children 12 to 17 years old　_____

　　　Adults 18 years old or older　_____

7c. How old is the *youngest* child in your household?

　　　_____ years old

8. Are you now: (Circle one number)

　　　Working at a full-time job 1

　　　Working at a part-time job 2

　　　Not working but looking for a job 3

　　　Not working and not looking for a job 4

If you are now working either full-time or part-time, answer the questions in the box below. If you are not working, go to Question 10.

9a. What do you do on this job? Please tell what you do most of the time.

　　　_____

　　　_____

　　　_____

　　　_____

　　　_____

9b. How long have you had this job?

　　　_____ months _____ years

9c. How many hours do you usually work each week?

　　　_____ hours a week

9d. Are you able to work as many days each week as you want to on this job?

　　　Yes 1

　　　No 0

9e. How much take-home pay do you usually get in a week?

　　　$_____ a week

9f. Do you get a paid vacation on this job?

　　　Yes 1

　　　No 0

9g. Do you get any paid sick leave on this job?

　　　Yes 1

　　　No 0

9h. Do you get health insurance on this job?

　　　Yes 1

　　　No 0

9i. Do you belong to a union on this job?

　　　Yes 1

　　　No 0

9j. How good a chance is there for advancement in this job?

　　　No chance at all 1

　　　Not much chance 2

　　　Fairly good chance 3

　　　Very good chance 4

9k. How much pride do you take in your work on this job?

　　　None at all 1

　　　Not much 2

　　　A fair amount 3

　　　A lot 4

9l. Overall, how much do you like this job?

　　　Not at all 1

　　　A little bit 2

　　　Fairly much 3

　　　Very much 4

If you have ever had a job before (not counting the job you might have now), answer the questions in the box below. If you have never had a job before now, go to Question 11.

10a. What did you do on **your last job?** Please tell what you did most of the time.

_____

_____

_____

_____

_____

10b. How long did you have that job?

_____ months _____ years

10c. How many hours did you usually work each week?

_____ hours a week

10d. Were you able to work as many days each week as you wanted to on that job?

Yes 1

No 0

10e. How much take-home pay did you usually get in a week?

$_____ a week

10f. Did you get a paid vacation on that job?

Yes 1

No 0

10g. Did you get any paid sick leave on that job?

Yes 1

No 0

10h. Did you get health insurance on that job?

Yes 1

No 0

10i. Did you belong to a union on that job?

Yes 1

No 0

10j. How good a chance was there for advancement in that job?

No chance at all 1

Not much chance 2

Fairly good chance 3

Very good chance 4

10k. How much pride did you take in your work on that job?

None at all 1

Not much 2

A fair amount 3

A lot 4

10l. Overall, how much did you like that job?

Not at all 1

A little bit 2

Fairly much 3

Very much 4

10m. How long ago did you leave that job?

_____ months _____ years

10n. Why did you leave that job?

Laid off 1

Fired 2

Company closed 3

Got a new job 4

Quit 5

Went on strike 6

Other _____

(Please describe)

10o. How did you feel about leaving that job?

Very bad 1

Fairly bad 2

Fairly good 3

Very good 4

11. How many different jobs have you had over the **past 5 years** — that is, since the Summer of 1973.

No jobs 0

_____ jobs

12. Which one statement best describes your work activities over the **past 5 years.**

a. I never worked at all 1

b. I worked less than half of that time 2

c. I worked about half of that time 3

d. I worked almost all of that time 4

e. I worked all of that time 5

13. How many months in the **past 5 years** were you not working but looking for work?

_____ months

14. How many months in the **past 5 years** were you not working and not looking for work?

_____ months

15. How many months in the **past 5 years** were you receiving welfare?

_____ months

16. How many months in the **past 5 years** were you receiving unemployment compensation?

_____ months

Circle the number next to each statement that best says how likely you are to be doing that activity at this time next year.

At this time next year how likely is it that you will be:	Not At All Likely	Not Too Likely	Fairly Likely	Very Likely
17a. Working at a full-time job	1	2	3	4
17b. Staying home to look after your family	1	2	3	4
17c. Receiving welfare	1	2	3	4
17d. Working at a part-time job	1	2	3	4
17e. Receiving unemployment compensation	1	2	3	4
17f. Looking for a job	1	2	3	4

If you expect to be working at a job at this time next year, answer questions in the box below. If not, go to Question 19.

At this time next year I expect to be working at a job:	Strongly Disagree	Disagree	Agree	Strongly Agree
18a. Where I earn enough to support my family	1	2	3	4
18b. That my family respects	1	2	3	4
18c. Where I could be laid off at any time	1	2	3	4
18d. Where I do the kind of work I like	1	2	3	4
18e. Where there is a chance for advancement	1	2	3	4
18f. That is the kind of job I would like my children to have when they grow up	1	2	3	4
18g. Where I get a paid vacation	1	2	3	4
18h. Where I get paid sick leave	1	2	3	4
18i. Where I get health insurance	1	2	3	4
18j. Where I belong to a union	1	2	3	4

If you have just applied for welfare or are now receiving welfare, answer the questions in the box below. If not, go to Question 20.

19a. Are you now on welfare? . . . . Yes 1

No 0

19b. If you are now on welfare, how long have you been on welfare? . . . . . _____ months _____ years

19c. Were you ever on welfare before this time? . . . . Yes 1

No 0

19d. Think about how you felt when you applied for welfare this time. Circle the number next to each statement that best describes how you felt.

	Strongly Disagree	Disagree	Agree	Strongly Agree
When I applied for welfare this time, I felt that:				
1. It was a big shock to have to apply for welfare 1	2	3	4
2. I could get more money on welfare than I could working full-time 1	2	3	4
3. If it weren't for welfare, my family would have a lot of money problems . 1	2	3	4
4. I would rather be on welfare than work to support my family 1	2	3	4
5. Getting welfare money would make things easier for my family 1	2	3	4
6. I could not earn enough at work to support my family 1	2	3	4

19e. Listed below are services that one might wish to have through the Work Incentive Program (WIN). Please circle one number next to each statement below which best says how much you would like to receive each service through WIN.

	Not At All	Not Too Much	Fairly Much	Very Much
I would like to receive these WIN services:				
1. More education. 1	2	3	4
2. Vocational training. 1	2	3	4
3. On the job training 1	2	3	4
4. Advice about getting a job 1	2	3	4
5. Placement in a regular job 1	2	3	4
6. Help with child care arrangements. 1	2	3	4
7. Counselling about my personal affairs 1	2	3	4
8. Sympathy about my situation 1	2	3	4
9. Enough money for work related expenses 1	2	3	4
10. Help in transportation to a job 1	2	3	4

19f. How much longer do you think you will be on welfare? . . . . _____ months _____ years

If you have just applied for unemployment compensation or are now receiving unemployment compensation, answer the questions in the box below. If not, go to Question 21.

20a. Are you now on unemployment compensation?   Yes 1
                                                         No 0

20b. If you are now receiving unemployment compensation, how long
      have you been receiving it?   _____ weeks _____ months

20c. Have you ever received unemployment compensation before now? Yes 1
                                                         No 0

20d. Think about how you felt when you applied for unemployment compensation this time. Circle the number next to
      each statement that best describes how you felt.

		Strongly Disagree	Disagree	Agree	Strongly Agree
When I applied for unemployment compensation this time, I felt that:					
1.	It was a big shock to me to have to apply for unemployment compensation 1		2	3	4
2.	I could get more money on unemployment compensation than I could working full-time 1		2	3	4
3.	If it weren't for unemployment compensation, my family would have a lot of money problems 1		2	3	4
4.	I would rather be on unemployment compensation than work to support my family 1		2	3	4
5.	Getting unemployment compensation money would make things easier for my family 1		2	3	4
6.	I could not earn enough at work to support my family 1		2	3	4

20e. How much longer do you think you will be on unemployment compensation? _____ weeks _____ months

---

21. How healthy would you say you are?

      In good health 1
      In average health 2
      In poor health 3

22. Do you have any specific health problems that might
     keep you from working regularly?

      Yes 1
      No 0

23. Do you have anyone to take care of your children
     while you are working?

      Yes 1
      No 0

24. Have you ever been unable to take a job because you
     could not find anyone to take care of your children?

      Yes 1
      No 0

25. How many adults in your household other than
     yourself are now working at full-time jobs?

      _____ adults working full-time

26. How many adults in your household other than
     yourself are now working at part-time jobs?

      _____ adults working part-time

27. About how much was your total household income last year before taxes?

    Less than $3,000 1

    $3,000 to $4,999 2

    $5,000 to $6,999 3

    $7,000 to $8,999 4

    $9,000 to $10,999 5

    $11,000 to $12,999 6

    $13,000 to $14,999 7

    $15,000 to $17,999 8

    $18,000 to $19,999 9

    $20,000 to $24,999 10

    $25,000 to $29,999 11

    $30,000 or more 12

28. Please circle each source of support that your family receives.

    Social security 1

    Food stamps 2

    Public housing 3

    Alimony or child support 4

    None of the above 5

29. Who owns the place you live in?

    I own it 1

    My mate owns it 2

    My mate and I both own it 3

    Another relative owns it 4

    Someone else owns the house 5

30. Do you or someone in your household own a car?

    Yes 1

    No 0

31. What language do you speak most often at home?

    Chinese 1

    English 2

    French 3

    Italian 4

    Polish 5

    Spanish 6

    Other _____ 7
                              (please name)

THANK YOU FOR YOUR HELP.

Appendix D
Validity of Results

The general purpose of this appendix is to raise and answer questions about the validity of results reported in the text. The questions are grouped under three headings as follows:

1. *Honesty of Response*. How do we know that respondents answered the survey questions honestly? Perhaps they just checked off answers at random or else biased their responses toward what they believed middle-class persons wished to hear.
2. *Validity of the Models*. How do we know that the economic independence models are valid and stable? Perhaps the models only represent the transient reponses of persons and would not be repeated at a different time.
3. *Generality of Results*. How do we know that the reinterviewed respondents (the ones who were interviewed both in 1978 and 1979) are representative of those who were not reinterviewed? Perhaps the non-reinterviewed persons are totally different from those who were located for the 1979 reinterview.

The following sections provide reasonable evidence on these questions.

Honesty of Response

If respondents to the questionnaires were answering at random, there would be no pattern to their ratings on the statements dealing with attitudes, beliefs, and expectations. The fact that definite patterns are observed—that is, items cluster together to form orientations that have psychological meaning (see Appendix B for details on the clustering procedure)—suggests that persons are answering in a thoughtful and consistent manner.

This finding does not preclude the possibility that respondents were systematically biasing their answers on the questionnaire. If welfare respondents were answering in terms of middle-class values or what middle-class persons wished to hear, we would expect to find certain patterns of results.

For example, we would expect welfare persons to give low ratings to items expressing preference for welfare. In fact, they give relatively high ratings. The mean value given to acceptance of welfare, as seen in table D–1, is significantly higher for welfare mothers than for UI mothers. We should find welfare mothers expressing high expectations of economic independence if they wished to impress middle-class persons. Instead, expectation of economic independence is significantly lower for welfare mothers compared to UI mothers. There is no evidence in the mean values of orientations (or background characteristics) to suggest that welfare persons are covering up their true feelings.

But how do we know that welfare respondents are not distorting their responses so that preference for income-support orientations do not appear as predictors of economic independence? It is virtually impossible for a large group of persons to know how to distort their answers on a large number of statements so as to affect a multiple-regression equation in a specific way, given the complexity of the interaction among variables that takes place in the formulation of that equation. The next section provides further evidence on the trustworthiness and validity of results from this study.

Validity of the Statistical Model of Economic Independence

A major concern of this book has been to elucidate the factors causing recipients of an income-support program to achieve economic independence. The usual variables measured by economists and sociologists, such as persons' earnings, other household income, and income support payments, are related to persons' level of economic independence, but are not direct measures of such independence. Needed is some way of combining the traditional variables to obtain a direct measure of independence.

Our approach is to view economic independence through work as a combination of the three variables that comprise total family income: extent of income support received; extent of one's own earnings through work; and extent of other household income. The values of economic independence obtained from combining these three sources of income in some fashion are to be continuous, with the lowest value occurring when there is complete dependence upon an income-support program. The values are to increase rapidly as income support goes down and own earnings or other income or both go up. Scores of a person with no income support are to go up as his own earnings become greater than other sources of household income.

A specific way of determining persons' scores on this continuous economic-independence scale can be computed by using the following definitions and equation:

Table D–1
Selected Orientations of WIN and UI Mothers
(means, standard deviations in parentheses)

| | 1978 Mean Values For Total Interviewed in 1978 | | 1978 Mean Values For Mothers Reinterviewed in 1979 | |
| | WIN Mothers | UI Mothers | WIN Mothers | UI Mothers |
Orientations	(n = 814)	(n = 245)	(n = 428)	(n = 141)
I. Expectations				
Expect Economic	2.89[a]	3.35	2.84[b]	3.31
Independence Through	- (0.79)	(0.60)	(0.74)	(0.61)
Work Next Year				
II. Preference for Nonwork Income				
5. Welfare Preferred To	1.64[c]	NA[d]	1.55	NA
Work	(0.77)		(0.72)	
6. UI Preferred to Work	NA	1.62[e]	NA	1.51
		(0.78)		(0.71)
8. Accept Welfare	2.36[a,c]	1.87	2.45[b]	1.93
When Necessary	(0.84)	(0.85)	(0.78)	(0.82)
10. Accept Government	2.48[a,c]	2.35	2.59[b]	2.43
Support When	(0.68)	(0.63)	(0.60)	(0.58)
Necessary				
12. Accept Social	2.52[c]	2.52	2.61	2.58
Security or Pension	(0.78)	(0.81)	(0.73)	(0.75)
When Necessary				
III. Normative Beliefs about Work, Family, and Government Support				
15. Father Should Leave	1.91[c]	1.83	1.78	1.77
Family If He Cannot	(0.62)	(0.63)	(0.54)	(0.60)
Support Them				
17. Family or Neighbors	2.08[a]	2.22[e]	2.06	2.12
Look Down On Me	(0.51)	(0.58)	(0.51)	(0.57)
For Receiving				
Welfare Or UI				
IV. Family Relationships				
21. Want Others, Not A	1.65[c]	1.61[e]	1.57	1.51
Husband, To Support	(0.66)	(0.54)	(0.49)	(0.45)
Your Family				
V. Self				
28. Success Through	2.40[c]	2.40	2.31	2.37
External Forces	(0.62)	(0.63)	(0.60)	(0.61)

[a]The mean given by total 1978 interviewed WIN mothers is significantly different from the mean given by total 1978 interviewed UI mothers (at the 0.01 level of probability).

[b]The mean given by reinterviewed WIN mothers is significantly different from the mean given by reinterviewed UI mothers (at the 0.01 level of probability).

[c]The mean given by the non-reinterviewed WIN mothers in 1978 is significantly different from the mean given by the WIN mothers in 1978 who were later reinterviewed. The means of the non-reinterviewed mothers are not given directly in the table to conserve space. These means can be derived from the means for the total group and the reinterviewed group.

[d]Data are not available or missing.

[e]The mean given by the non-reinterviewed UI mothers in 1978 is significantly different from the mean given by the UI mothers in 1978 who were later reinterviewed. The means of the non-reinterviewed mothers are not given directly in the table to conserve space. These means can be derived from the means for the total group and the reinterviewed group.

1. %OWN   = percentage of total income from own earnings
2. %SUPPORT = percentage of total income from income-support
                 programs
3. %OTHER   = percentage of total income from other household
                 sources of income
4. %SUPPORT + %OWN + %OTHER = 100%
5. (ECONOMIC INDEPENDENCE $= \dfrac{(\%\text{own})}{100}\,(100 - \%\text{other})$
   THROUGH WORK)^2

$- (\%\text{support})(100 - \%\text{own})$

The value of Economic Independence is the square root of the number obtained from equation 5 if that number is positive. If the number is negative, Economic Independence is the negative value of the square root of the absolute value of the number obtained from equation 5. Economic Independence values will vary from -100 to $+10$. This nonlinear but continuous description of economic independence indicates that people who are on a support program with no other source of income are much further away from economic independence than people who have other sources of income, especially their own earnings. The equation also says that economic-independence levels of people who are *not* on an income-support program are not vastly different from one another. (In our calculation of the continuous variable, others' earnings in the household was used for income from other sources.)

A much simpler and more intuitively obvious variable can be used conveniently as a substitute for this more complex, continuous measure of economic independence. The correlation between the simpler four-point measure (ECOI) described in chapter 2 and the measure presented in equation 5 is very high: 0.95 for the WIN mothers and the WIN fathers. Moreover, the same independent variables that predict the four-point measure (ECOI) for WIN mothers or WIN fathers also predict the continuous measure. The only differences are slight changes in the beta weights.

Given the fact that a measure of economic independence is not generally used by social scientists, it is important to show that the model predicting economic independence is reasonable. One way of doing this is to show that the model obtained is similar to that obtained for related but more traditional dependent variables.

One of the more traditional dependent variables is created by collapsing the four-point scale of the simplified economic independence measure (ECOI) into a two-point scale. That is, by combining the zero and 1 scores into one rating and the 2 and 3 scores into another rating, we have a dichotomous dependent variable indicating whether one is on or off welfare at the time of reinterview. When the model predicting economic independence is applied to this new dependent variable, using a probit analysis because of the dichotomous dependent variable, all the independent variables remain significant. This finding is true for WIN mothers or WIN fathers. (These data are available from the author on request.)

A second traditional dependent variable is average earnings of WIN mothers or WIN fathers during the 1977–1978 period. The application of the economic-independence model to average earnings of each of these groups shows that virtually all of the variables predicting economic independence hold for this familiar dependent variable as well.[1] Hence, there is reason to believe that the economic-independence variable we constructed is reasonable and useful and that the model which predicts it is valid.

It also is useful to examine the relevance of the economic-independence model for predicting the dependent variable termed "work related to economic independence" (WECOI). WECOI is similar to economic independence except the 1 and 2 ratings have been reversed, giving emphasis to whether one is working or not, rather than whether one is on an income-support program or not, as follows:

Economic Independence Through Work (ECOI)	Work Relate to Economic Independence (WECOI)
0 = Yes income support, No work	0 = Yes income support, No work
1 = Yes income support, Yes work	1 = No income support, No work
2 = No income support, No work	2 = Yes income support, Yes work
3 = No income support, Yes work	3 = No income support, Yes work

The same models that predict economic independence for WIN mothers and WIN fathers also predicts work related to economic independence. Getting a job through WIN contributes much more to the explanation of WECOI than to ECOI for the mothers. This finding suggests that the WIN-obtained job gets mothers more readily into the work force than it allows them to become independent of an income-support program. Data supporting these conclusions are presented elsewhere.[2] The point is that the variables which predict economic independence are the same as those which predict work related to economic independence.

The variables included in the final economic independence models, as explained in the appendix to chapter 3, had to be significant in both the ordinary least-squares (OLS) analysis and the tobit analysis. That dual procedure provided some assurance of the models being stable, containing only variables that were indeed significant predictors of economic independence. To ensure even greater stability, it was decided further that only those variables would be included in the final model which also predicted economic independence two months prior to the reinterview. This was possible because respondents during the reinterview were asked to indicate on a month-by-month basis their employment, welfare, and UI experiences for the period between interviews.

Month-by-Month Predictions for WIN Mothers

From the month-by-month data on income sources, an economic-independence measure was constructed for each respondent for each month between the two interviews. The predictor variables used in the economic-independence model were then applied to each of these other economic-independence measures. Table D–2 presents these results for WIN mothers.

Two points are clear from this table. First, there is a continuing flow of mothers from welfare toward economic independence over the twelve-month period—for example, there is a decline of those in total dependence from 83 percent to 65 percent. Second, the economic independence model becomes stronger as time goes on, as seen in the significance levels of the predictor variables and the R^2 values. These findings indicate that the results for WIN mothers presented in the text have general applicability over time and are not the result of a transient situation at time of reinterview. A similar pattern of results occurs for WIN fathers. (These data are presented elsewhere to conserve space.[3])

The two predictive expectations for WIN mothers (orientation 1 and item 2c) are statistically significant throughout the eleven-month period as well as at the time of reinterview. Thus, expectations about independence have a continuing effect upon persons' efforts to achieve that result. At the same time, we have seen that the experience of success markedly affects these expectations. How are we to account for both the stability and changeability of orientations? One might think of these expectations as comprising a durable and a changeable component. That is, over the years persons develop a more or less fixed level of expectation. But then immediate experience has an additional impact on these

Table D–2
Applying the Economic-Independence (ECOI) Model for WIN Mothers Month by Month (1978–1979)

Independent Variables	Months Since Initial 1978 Interview											Reinterview
	1	2	3	4	5	6	7	8	9	10	11	12 (ECOI)[a]
1. Expect Economic Independence through Work Next Year—Female	2.9	3.0	2.7	3.2	3.1	3.6	3.8	4.1	3.9	3.9	3.2	3.8
2c. Expect to be Looking for Job Next Year	-3.2	-3.9	-4.4	-4.2	-3.9	-4.2	-4.0	-4.2	-3.6	-3.7	-3.6	-3.3
12. Accept Social Security	1.3	1.5	1.3	1.9	1.9	1.4	0.7	1.1	1.8	2.0	2.6	2.5
24. Family Satisfaction (Blacks only)	1.8	1.5	1.8	1.3	1.2	1.4	2.0	2.7	2.9	4.1	2.8	3.3
Months On Welfare 1973–1978	-3.3	-2.4	-3.0	-3.1	-3.7	-4.2	-3.9	-3.5	-3.8	-3.8	-3.8	-3.9
Previous Job Status	3.0	3.9	3.6	3.0	3.0	1.8	1.7	2.1	2.2	2.2	2.0	2.1
R^2 (adjusted) Background Characteristics[b]	0.09	0.09	0.10	0.09	0.10	0.09	0.08	0.08	0.09	0.09	0.10	0.10
R^2 (adjusted) Orientations[b]	0.04	0.05	0.05	0.06	0.05	0.06	0.06	0.08	0.07	0.09	0.09	0.10
R^2 (adjusted) Total[b]	0.13	0.14	0.15	0.15	0.15	0.15	0.14	0.16	0.16	0.18	0.19	0.20
Percentage Distribution of ECOI Scores by Month												
0 = Yes income support, No work	83	78	76	74	73	70	70	69	69	68	68	65
1 = Yes income support, Yes work	6	11	12	13	14	15	13	14	12	13	13	14
2 = No income support, No work	4	3	2	3	3	3	3	3	3	3	4	5
3 = No income support, Yes work	6	8	10	11	10	12	14	14	16	16	15	16
Total Percentage	99	100	100	101	100	100	100	100	100	100	100	100
Total Number Responding	416	415	415	415	415	415	415	415	414	414	402	417

Table D–2 Continued

Independent Variables	Months Since Initial 1978 Interview											Reinterview
	1	2	3	4	5	6	7	8	9	10	11	12 (ECOI)[a]
Correlation of ECOI with Economic Independence Measures Month-by-month	0.48	0.55	0.55	0.58	0.61	0.64	0.73	0.79	0.84	0.89	0.93	—

Note: Each column contains the t ratio for the variables in the model that predict economic independence. The t ratios are associated with the coefficient of each independent variable as obtained from a multiple-regression equation in which the dependent variable was the economic independence score for that month. Each underlined t ratio indicates a probability of 0.10 or less of that variable being nonsignificant in the equation.

[a]The values in this column are taken from table 3A–1.

[b]The R^2 values have been obtained by entering Race and City first in the stepwise multiple regression equation, then followed by the background characteristics, and finally by the orientations. This procedure provides a minimum estimate of the effect of the orientations and a maximum estimate of the effect of background characteristics. Total R^2 is the sum of the R^2 for background characteristics and orientations.

orientations. The practical implication of such a viewpoint is that one cannot expect immediate experience to revolutionize totally a person's expectations—either totally dash them if there are negative experiences or raise them extremely high if there are positive experiences. More research is needed to test and clarify this interpretation.

The two other orientations in the economic-independence model—accept social security or pension and family satisfaction—are significant predictors for only the later months of the 1978–1979 period. Certain orientations may affect action only after a period of time or after other experiences have occurred. Here again further research is needed on the impact of orientations on action over time.

The fact that "months on welfare 1973–1978" is a significant predictor throughout the twelve-month period needs to be seen in light of its predictors (see note 2, chapter 3). The strongest predictor is previous job pay. Factors that made it unlikely for one to get a high-paying job in the long-term past (prior to 1978) continue to affect one's ability to achieve economic independence in the short-term past (1978–1979) and in the present. The same argument can be used to account for previous job status being a significant predictor of economic independence over the months.

Month-by-Month Predictors for UI Mothers

It is of special interest to consider how the model for economic independence in 1979 applies to the month-by-month measures of economic independence for UI mothers. Table D–3 presents this information, following the same organization of material as for WIN mothers. Most noteworthy, the model is virtually useless for the first five months between interviews, but does predict about 0.05 of the variance during the sixth to ninth months. During the tenth and eleventh months, all three predictor variables are significant in the regression equation and predict about 0.10 of the variance in economic independence scores.

This pattern is explainable by the fact that UI benefits tend to last for six months. There is, in fact, a sharp decrease in dependency during the seventh month following the initial interview. (This same kind of decrease in dependency during the seventh month is noted for UI fathers in data not presented here.) What appears to be happening is that many persons are staying on the benefit program during the initial six months regardless of their background characteristics or orientations. As benefits come to an end, persons begin efforts to move back into the work force. Background characteristics and orientations then play a strong role in affecting the level of economic independence achieved by UI mothers.

Table D–3

Applying the Economic-Independence (ECOI) Model for UI Mothers Month by Month (1978–1979)

| Independent Variables | Months Since Initial 1978 Interview | | | | | | | | | | | Reinterview |
	1	2	3	4	5	6	7	8	9	10	11	12 (ECOI)[a]
1. Expect Economic Independence through Work Next Year—												
Female	-1.0	-0.7	-0.6	-0.6	1.1	1.9	3.1	3.5	3.5	3.8	4.0	2.8
9. Accept UI when Necessary	-1.1	-1.4	-0.6	-0.7	-2.0	-2.1	-1.6	-1.3	-0.9	-1.8	-1.6	-2.6
Previous Job Pay ($/week)	0.9	2.0	1.0	0.3	0.5	1.2	0.7	0.4	0.3	2.2	2.2	2.8
R^2 (adjusted) Background Characteristics[b]	0.00	0.01	0.00	0.00	0.00	0.00	0.00	0.00	0.00	0.02	0.02	0.03
R^2 (adjusted) Orientations[b]	0.00	0.00	0.00	0.00	0.02	0.04	0.06	0.07	0.06	0.09	0.09	0.07
R^2 (adjusted) Total[b]	0.00	0.01	0.00	0.00	0.02	0.04	0.06	0.07	0.06	0.11	0.11	0.10
Percentage Distribution of ECOI Scores by Month												
0 = Yes income support, No work	61	56	48	48	44	42	31	26	27	28	28	27
1 = Yes income support, Yes work	6	8	8	7	9	5	6	6	6	5	5	5
2 = No income support, No work	20	16	16	14	14	15	21	23	19	18	21	22
3 = No income support, Yes work	14	21	28	31	34	37	41	45	48	48	45	46
Total Percentage	101	101	100	100	101	99	99	100	100	99	99	100
Total Number Responding	140	140	140	140	140	139	140	140	139	137	110	140
Correlation of ECOI with Economic Independence Measures Month-by-month	0.17	0.23	0.28	0.33	0.45	0.61	0.72	0.76	0.78	0.85	0.89	—

Note: Each column contains the *t* ratio for the variables in the model that predict economic independence. The *t* ratios are associated with the coefficient of each independent variable as obtained from a multiple-regression equation in which the dependent variable was the economic independence score for that month. Each *italicized t* ratio indicates a probability of 0.10 or less of that variable being nonsignificant in the equation.

[a]The values in this column are taken from table 3A–2.

[b]The R^2 values have been obtained by entering Race, City, and whether mother received welfare or not first in the stepwise multiple-regression equation, then entering the background characteristics, and finally entering the orientations. This procedure provides a minimum estimate of the effect of the orientations and a maximum estimate of the effect of background characteristics. Total R^2 is the sum of R^2 for background characteristics and orientations.

These findings and interpretations suggest that there may be a significant amount of malingering on the UI program—persons staying on when they could in fact find employment or live on other resources. This kind of pattern is not observed for WIN mothers or WIN fathers.

An interpretation of these findings is presented in chapter 7. The point of major significance here is that there are strong reasons to believe that our measure of economic independence through work and the models predicting it for the several groups are valid and stable.

Generality of Results

One way of judging whether the reinterviewed persons are similar to those who were not reinterviewed is to compare the background characteristics of the two groups. There is no statistically significant difference (0.01 level of probability) between reinterviewed and non-reinterviewed UI mothers. There is a single difference for WIN mothers: those reinterviewed spent a few more months on welfare during the 1973–1978 period than those not reinterviewed (37.6 months versus 33.4 months). These data on background characteristics are presented elsewhere.[4]

There are a few differences in orientations between those reinterviewed and not reinterviewed, as seen in table D–1. The differences for WIN mothers center around acceptance of welfare. There is, however, no consistent pattern among the orientations. For example, although non-reinterviewed WIN mothers are less accepting of welfare income when necessary, they are more in favor of welfare over work. Of most importance, there are no significant differences between non-reinterviewed and reinterviewed mothers with respect to expectation of economic independence and working next year.

There is some indication that non-reinterviewed UI mothers are more accepting of income support than reinterviewed mothers, based on differences between two orientations. But given the similarities regarding the many other orientations, there is little reason to regard the two groups as different. Similar conclusions can be drawn from data presented elsewhere on the reinterviewed and non-reinterviewed WIN and UI fathers.[5]

Next Steps in Testing Validity

It is important to recognize that the statistical arguments just made are only an intermediate step in the validation of the models developed in this study. Further steps are required. They could involve other studies aimed at replicating or refuting the results of the present study. More significantly, they could involve a practical program of training and job opportunities coupled with a sophisticated research effort to determine whether the program actually raised expectations and self-support activities of poor people, increased the number of two-parent families, and markedly lowered the welfare rolls. A broad effort of that kind not only would test the findings of the present study but would provide new information about ways to expand opportunities for poor people to maintain their economic independence. These possibilities are outlined in chapter 7.

Notes

1. Leonard Goodwin, *The Impact of Federal Income Security Programs on Work Incentives and Marital Stability* (Worcester, Mass.: Worcester Polytechnic Institute, 1981), pp. 4–55, 5–46.
2. Ibid., pp. 4–55 to 4–57.
3. Ibid., p. 5–40.
4. Ibid., pp. 4–3 to 4–7.
5. Ibid., pp. 5–2 to 5–4.

Index

About the Author

Leonard Goodwin is professor and head of the Department of Social Science and Policy Studies at Worcester Polytechnic Institute. Previously he was on the staff of Brookings Institution in Washington, D.C. He has written extensively on issues of public welfare, social psychology of the poor, and policy research, and is the author of two previous books: *Do the Poor Want To Work?* (1972) and *Can Social Science Help Resolve National Problems?* (1975).

DATE DUE